Leading the Customer Experience

Leading the Customer Experience

Inspirational Service Leadership

SARAH COOK

GOWER

Published by
Gower Publishing Limited
Wey Court East
Union Road
Farnham
Surrey, GU9 7PT
England

Gower Publishing Company
110 Cherry Street
Suite 3-1
Burlington, VT 05401-3818
USA

www.gowerpublishing.com

British Library Cataloguing in Publication Data
A catalogue record for this book is available from the British Library

Library of Congress Cataloging-in-Publication Data
Cook, Sarah, 1955-
  Leading the customer experience : inspirational service leadership / by Sarah Cook.
    pages cm
  Includes bibliographical references and index.
  ISBN 978-1-4724-4769-2 (hardback) -- ISBN 978-1-4724-4770-8 (ebook) -- ISBN 978-1-4724-4771-5 (epub) 1. Customer services. 2. Leadership. 3. Customer relations. I. Title.
  HF5415.5.C66355 2015
  658.8'12--dc23

2015005298

ISBN: 9781472447692 (hbk)
ISBN: 9781472447708 (ebk – ePDF)
ISBN: 9781472447715 (ebk – ePUB)

Printed in the United Kingdom by Henry Ling Limited, at the Dorset Press, Dorchester, DT1 1HD

Contents

List of Figures

Acknowledgements

Very special thanks to my colleague and friend Hilary Coldicott who has helped me compile much of the material in this book. I could not have done it without you.

Also to my friend Steve Macaulay from Cranfield School of Management with whom I have written many articles on customer experience over the years and who shares my passion for customer excellence.

Preface

Hello and welcome to *Leading the Customer Experience*. Thank you for choosing to read this book and to join the community of practitioners who recognize the importance of leadership in delivering exceptional service.

Most organization's strategic aims and goals centre on retaining and gaining customers via the delivery of an excellent customer experience. We know that loyal customers not only keep buying from a company but also recommend the business to others.

Having worked in the field of customer experience for some time, it is clear that managers and leaders throughout an organization have a key influence on the experience that customers receive. How leaders behave has a direct impact on their team member's motivation to go the extra mile to deliver excellent service for the customer and the extent to which they feel empowered to make the right decision for the customer.

My vision for *Leading the Customer Experience* is to provide practical advice, tools and techniques for managers in how to effectively lead and motivate their team to deliver the best possible customer experience.

There has been much written around the topic of leadership, but little if anything specifically about leadership in a service organization. At The Stairway Consultancy we specialize in customer and employee engagement. We have extensively researched the behaviours of leaders who successfully create an environment where employees deliver exceptional service. This book encapsulates the work myself and The Stairway Consultancy team have undertaken globally over a number years around the practicalities of how leaders role-model customer-centricity.

My intention is to provide a pragmatic and business-focused approach to the topic using practical examples, case studies and research about how to effectively lead and engender an organizational culture that is customer-focused. We have included checklists and recommended actions as guides at the end of each chapter. These will help you assess your own leadership behaviours and apply ideas, tools and techniques to facilitate the delivery of exceptional service in your organization.

Sarah Cook

The Stairway Consultancy
sarah@thestairway.co.uk

Chapter 1

Why Does Leadership Matter When it Comes to Customer Experience?

In this introductory chapter we look at:

- What is exceptional customer experience?

- The increasing power of the customer

- The benefits of delivering exceptional service

- Employee engagement and customer engagement

- The role leaders play in creating a customer-focused environment

You will find tips and ideas, self-assessments and checklists throughout this book to help you reflect and develop your and others' role as a customer leader. At the end of each chapter there are also suggested actions you can take as a leader based on the key learning points.

Exceptional Customer Experience and Customer Engagement

Think of a time when you have been impressed by the service you have received from an organization. It could be online, face-to-face or on the phone. Chances are that you can recall an exceptional customer experience. You probably also can remember just as vividly, if not more, a poor experience where your expectations were not met. The way our brain works means that we have a tendency to more likely remember the negatives rather than the positives. In fact for every one negative experience, we need 12 positive customer experiences for the negative to fade away.

As customers we buy based on emotions as well as logic. The more we receive exceptional service as a customer of an organization, the more we become emotionally engaged with the brand. Customer engagement is not something that happens by chance, but is rather an outcome of an exceptional and differentiated customer experience.

Engaged customers are loyal to a business and customer loyalty has long been linked to profitability and growth. Engaged customers buy more from a company, lessening the cost to serve. If they like what you do, they'll talk about it. They'll recommend your service. Nothing is more powerful and authentic than a peer referral or word-of-mouth marketing. Engaged customers are passionate about the organization. They love what you do and they'll provide free peer-to-peer advertising to make sure it's known. Customer engagement improves your business revenues, opportunity for growth, your reputation and customer lifetime value.

THE WAY CUSTOMERS INTERACT WITH ORGANIZATIONS HAS CHANGED

However, driving high levels of customer engagement has become increasingly more challenging as the way customers interact with businesses changes. Fifty years ago most organizations adopted an industrialized approach to customer interaction:

- Centralized decision makers anticipated and shaped customers' needs

- Organizations treated people as passive consumers

- Detailed demand forecasts carefully scripted the actions organizations had with consumers

- Businesses focused on pushing product to large, loosely defined customer segments

- The approach many businesses took to their customers was: *'We know better than you do about what you need,'*

Fast-forward to today. Businesses have experienced a big shift from 'push' product-centred marketing to customers to a 'pull' approach which needs to be far more customer-centric. This has been brought about by factors such as:

- The revolution in digital infrastructure which has improved processing power, storage and data transport, cloud computing and mobile Internet access

- Government liberalization across countries and deregulation

- The economic shift – enhanced technology has reduced barriers to entry, making it much easier for customers to find information and switch suppliers

- Changing work life patterns and greater use of tablets and mobile phones which mean that customers are now connected 24 hours a day and require constant access to information

- Wider choice of communication channels from webchat to video phones, which means that customers want to interact with businesses in different ways.

- Informed buyers now taking control of the sales cycle

- Consumerization of business-to-business markets via increasing customer power.

The old-fashioned 'push' approach is one where organizations try to put product and services in front of customers who may or may not have knowledge of a company or realize they have a particular need, in an attempt to create demand.

With the advent of the digital age and social media, the 'pull' approach ensures that customers know who businesses are so when they have a need they know where to go to satisfy that need. This means that organizations must create advocates for their brands because the buying decision itself is often driven by the opinions of other customers, rather than what the organization says about itself:

- A recent survey for Consumer Focus found that more than 62 per cent of consumers trust what other consumers tell them more than what companies say

- Research by BT and Avaya found that 51 per cent trust the advice on review sites more than an organization's official website

- Research from the USA by Nielsen found that 68 per cent of social media users go to social networking sites to read consumer feedback on products and services, with over half using these sites to provide product feedback, both positive and negative. Nielsen research also found that 'recommendations from personal acquaintances or opinions posted by consumers online are the most trusted forms of advertising'

- A 2013 survey of Internet users in Britain by Reevoo found that 88 per cent of consumers consult reviews when making a purchase, and 60 per cent said they were more likely to purchase from a site that has customer reviews.

So the customer is more in charge of the buying process than ever before. This phenomenon is just as prevalent in the business-to-business sector as the business-to-consumer. Research by Sirius in the UK in 2013 found that business consumers were typically 57 per cent of the way through their purchase process before they contacted suppliers. The same research found that 45 per cent of business consumers had already consulted the Internet before speaking to the potential supplier, 24 per cent had spoken to team members and colleagues about supplier options, 21 per cent had discussed options with a peer and 11 per cent had accessed online communities for reviews.

Reputation and trust therefore have become far more important in the customer's mind, as has the power of great service. As illustrated in Figure 1.1, further research by Sirius in 2013 found that brand reputation was driven 40 per cent by the product and price, 20 per cent via the quality of the processes used to interact with the organization and 40 per cent via the quality of the service the consumer receives.

Figure 1.1   Reputation

THE CHALLENGE OF CREATING CUSTOMER ADVOCACY

So service quality is playing an increasingly important role in the customer's eyes. The issue for many businesses is that research shows that while 80 per cent believe they are delivering a great service, only 8 per cent of their customers would agree. Paradoxically our experience shows that the larger and more seemingly successful a business is, the more remote it becomes from its customers and the less agile and less empowered employees are to anticipate and respond to customer needs. At the time of writing (April 2015), supermarket chain Tesco appears to be an example of a large corporate that has lost its way when it comes to customer experience.

AUTHENTIC SERVICE

The best customer engagement experience feels authentic for each customer but not in a one-size-fits-all fashion. Customers value a personal and individualized service that is tailored to their needs. Their degree of engagement is determined by the total sum of the experiences they have with the organization – at each touch point and via whatever channel they chose.

Customer engagement is also driven by consistent service. So for example, in the UK the telephone and online banking organization, First Direct, consistently tops the polls for customer satisfaction and retention year after year within the financial services sector, as the levels of service it provides remain constantly high in every customer interaction, irrespective of channel.

In order to deliver exceptional service an organization needs to provide a consistent service at three levels, as illustrated in Figure 1.2.

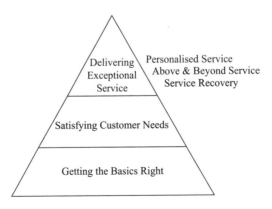

Figure 1.2   The Service Pyramid

GETTING THE BASICS RIGHT

As a service provider, you do not pass 'Go' in the customer's eyes unless you deliver the basic requirements of the service. The basics will be different for each type of organization. For an online retailer the basic requirements of the customer may be easy access to the site, the ability to easily navigate the site and being able to order goods and services in a speedy and hassle-free manner. For a restaurant or visitor attraction the basics may be clear signage, easy parking, access to clean toilet facilities, a warm welcome etc.

Often the basic elements of a service are the 'hygiene' factors that your business needs to get right in order to create a positive experience. They can be a mixture of physical and material elements such as product merchandising and opening hours, as well as things service employees do personally such as wear a uniform and/or meet and greet customers in a friendly manner.

The basics don't necessarily equate to increases in satisfaction when done well, but they invariably lead to complaints and dissatisfaction when done poorly. If an organization does not succeed at getting the basics right then the chances are that customers are likely to become detractors of the organization and the levels of complaints will rise. So the trick is to do the basics brilliantly.

SATISFYING THE CUSTOMER'S NEEDS

The next level of service centres on satisfying the customer's needs. For example a customer may need to have their car serviced: was the service carried out efficiently, on time and within the anticipated costs? Did the service organization meet the requirements that are important to the customer with minimal effort? An example for a train service could be whether the train ran on time, whether staff provided relevant information during the journey and the availability of staff at the station.

Customer requirements in this area generally relate to efficiency, reliability, quality, accuracy, knowledge and responsiveness. These factors help the service organization meet customers' requirements. However, they are not factors which will differentiate the experience in a way that adds value to the customer and gives them something they don't think they'll get elsewhere. They are not factors which excite or delight the customer.

DELIVERING EXCEPTIONAL SERVICE

The majority of customer experiences fall in to the 'satisfied' category. The customer has received the service they were expecting and they think no more about it. The experience does not engender loyalty to the organization and as a consequence the satisfied customer is unfaithful: they are just as likely to use other similar products and services that your competitors provide, and less likely than highly engaged customers to repeat buy your product, to increase their average transaction value and to recommend your service.

By going above and beyond what is expected by the customer, an organization can enhance the level of engagement that the customer feels towards the brand. Engagement goes beyond satisfaction. It is fundamentally about an emotional connection the customer feels to a business or a brand. When customers become emotionally engaged they are passionate about the organization; they become advocates and promoters for the brand.

Successful service organizations create customer advocacy in three ways:

1.   Personalized service: They offer a tailored, personal service that recognizes individual preferences and provides the customer with choices related to their needs. An example of this is how online retailer Amazon has created advocacy via its online service, remembering the products customers have bought in the past and making it easy to do business via its one-click option . Many organizations such as car retailer BMW remember the personal preferences of its customers so that they can individualize the service to each customer.

2.   Above and beyond service: they provide more than the customer expects – either in terms of the little extras it may provide the customer, such as a carry out service to the car, a thoughtful unexpected addition to the product or service, or most likely, where service personnel take the time to help the customer in ways that are unexpected. There are many examples of this, ranging from the bank clerk who takes responsibility to personally visit a housebound elderly customer with the forms she needs to sign rather than the customer having to come in to the bank, to the airline representative who offers to post a letter on their return to the country of origin on behalf of a customer who has forgotten to send off an important document.

3.   Service recovery: organizations with highly engaged customers take complaints seriously and realize the power of effective service recovery. This means ensuring that complaints are dealt with speedily, making it easy to complain and giving the customer the benefit of the doubt. (Research from my company, The Stairway Consultancy shows that the longer the customer has to wait for their complaint to be resolved, the less likely they are to be happy with the resolution. Global research company TARP has found that a customer who complains and whose complaint is dealt with well is more likely to remain loyal to the organization than those customers who do not complain at all (91 per cent loyalty versus 87 per cent loyalty for non-complaining customers).

These three drivers of customer engagement are not about what is being done, they are rather about the way it is done and how this differentiates the organization and builds sustainable competitive advantage.

So What is the Result of Exceptional Service?

If you or your colleagues still remain unconvinced of the need to take a lead when it comes to customer engagement, here is some empirical research which sets out more reasons why. Evidence points to increased levels of profitability and organizational growth when companies do well by their customers. As I have outlined earlier, they are rewarded by repeat business, lower price elasticity, higher repeat business, more cross-selling opportunities and greater marketing efficiency. Studies in the past 20 years indicate that the health of a business's customer relationships is a relevant indicator of their performance. This is irrespective of whether your organization is in the private, public or third sector, whether you are in the business-to-business or business-to-consumer sector.

High levels of customer satisfaction can reduce costs related to warranties, complaints, defective goods and service costs. Other evidence also suggests that if a customer perceives they are receiving superior quality, the company receives with higher economic returns. *Customer Centered Six Sigma: Linking Customers, Process Improvement, And Financial Results,* a study conducted in IBM Rochester by Naumann and Hoisington (2001) found positive associations between employee satisfaction, customer satisfaction, market share, and productivity.

In their seminal book *The Service Profit Chain* (1997) Heskett, Sasser and Schlesinger cite case-based research studies that demonstrate that customer satisfaction is positively associated with employee loyalty, cost competitiveness, profitable performance, and long-term growth. Their premise is that:

- Profit and growth are stimulated primarily by customer loyalty

- Loyalty is a direct result of customer satisfaction

- Satisfaction is largely influenced by the perceived value of services provided to customers

- Value is created by satisfied, loyal, and productive employees

- Employee satisfaction, in turn, results primarily from high-quality support services and policies that enable employees to deliver results to customers.

The service–profit chain (as illustrated in Figure 1.3) is also defined by a special kind of leadership that emphasizes the importance of each employee and customer. I'll discuss this in more detail later.

The service–profit chain research suggests that customer loyalty is the key determinant of profitability. The same research suggested that a 5 per cent improvement in customer loyalty results in a 25 to 85 per cent improvement in profits. In a study of the relationship between customer satisfaction and shareholder return, Anderson, Fornell, and Mazvancheryl's article Customer Satisfaction and Shareholder Value (2004) also found a strong relationship between customer satisfaction and shareholder value. So delivering excellent service makes sound economic sense; it also has a positive impact for employees.

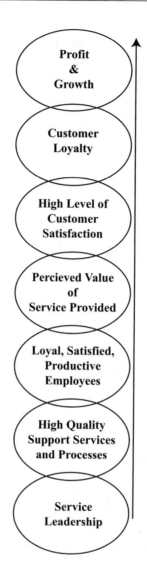

Figure 1.3   Service-Profit Chain

The Benefits of Excellent Service to the Employee

Organizations with a strong customer ethic are more likely to have engaged employees. When an organization embraces customer-centricity and this becomes part of the culture, chances are this produces a healthier and more motivational work environment for employees. Why is this?

Organizations with a customer-centric culture are more likely to listen to their external customers *and* their employees. The environment is likely to be more innovative and productive because its one where employees feel encouraged to give of their best. They get a buzz from serving the customer and their ideas and suggestions for improvement are actively sought, respected and implemented.

Service Excellence and Employee Engagement

Employee engagement has today become the holy grail of customer experience because it has been shown that customers who score the highest in customer engagement measures have experienced a service delivered by employees who in turn are highly engaged with their business.

In a study called *Linking People Measures to Strategy* by The Conference Board employees' customer service productivity scores and their employee engagement scores had a correlation of 0.51. In other words, engaged employees are more likely to deliver excellent service. Global research organization Gallup corroborated this fact in 2013 in its meta analysis *The Relationship Between Engagement at Work and Organizational Outcomes* when it found that businesses who are rated by customers as above average in terms of customer experience have 75 per cent of their employees who are highly or moderately engaged. This is compared to 34 per cent engagement levels in organizations which customers rate average or below.

Other evidence also points to the importance of employee engagement:

- A study of 23,910 business units compared top quartile and bottom quartile engagement scores and found that those in the top quartile averaged 12 per cent higher profitability. (*The Relationship Between Engagement at Work and Organizational Outcomes*)

- 5 per cent increase in total employee engagement correlates to a 0.7 per cent increase in operating margin (*European Talent Survey: Reconnecting with Employees: Attracting, Retaining, and Engaging, Towers Perrin*).

- Teams classified as in the 'high performance zone for engagement' had a 37 per cent Net Promoter Score (NPS) versus 10 per cent Net

Promoter Score (NPS) for teams 'outside of the high performance zone for engagement' (*Aon Hewitt European Manager Survey*).

- Highly engaged employees were 87 per cent less likely to leave their companies than their disengaged counterparts (*Driving Performance and Retention through Employee Engagement*).

Study of 89 companies compared top quartile and bottom quartile engagement scores and found that those in the top quartile had 2.6 times higher earnings per share (EPS) than that of the below-average scores Investors Take Note: Engagement Boosts Earnings Discretionary Effort

Let's now consider how customer engagement is driven by employee engagement. There are many definitions of employee engagement:

- 'An employee's drive to use all their ingenuity and resources for the benefit of the company'

- 'Aligning corporate agendas with personal motivation'

- 'Commitment to keep the brand promise'

- 'Loyalty – to a company, a brand or a customer'

- 'Taking your people with you'

My preferred definition is 'harnessing discretionary effort'. This is because it implies that employees have a choice in how they behave and whether they go out of their way to deliver 'above and beyond'.

Take organizations that constantly feature as top of their game for customer experience. For example in the UK, employee-owned department store John Lewis is often cited. I've certainly always experienced good service in John Lewis and consequently always promote their stores. The last time I went in to purchase some curtains, the partner I spoke to was knowledgeable and helpful. She took the time to listen and explain the different options and encouraged me to take home some samples free of charge to test. When I went back in store the partner recognized me and discussed my preferences, she was personable and individualized the service to my needs. The partner left me with the impression that nothing was too much trouble and she went above and beyond to exceed my expectations.

At the top of the service pyramid I referred to earlier, we see that to provide an exceptional customer experience involves the delivery of either a personalized service, an above and beyond service or effective service recovery. This delivery is dependent on having highly engaged and empowered employees who have the energy and the willingness to help the customer. The difference between a team member delivering exceptional versus satisfactory service is the degree to which they decide to expend discretionary effort. This is the crux of exceptional service. Are employees committed and willing to go the extra mile for the customer and do they have the energy and drive to see this through?

As a customer you can be dealt with in a similar service situation by two different people and experience two different customer interactions. The attitude and approach of each of the two service providers will vary according to whether each individual choses to deliver standard, satisfactory service or to go above and beyond. This is their personal choice and discretion. An organization cannot mandate that this should happen (though some command and control-type businesses unsuccessfully do). It is up to the employee whether they make the effort to personalise the service, to go above and beyond and/or to deliver exemplary service recovery.

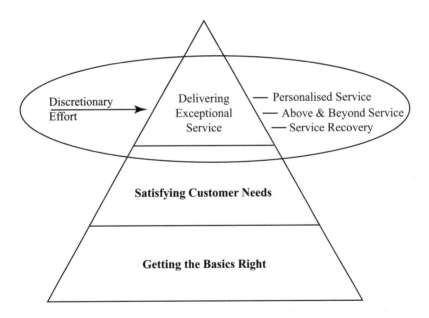

Figure 1.4   Discretionary Effort

HOW DO LEADERS CREATE ENGAGEMENT?

There are a number of factors that define engagement such as commitment to the organization, job satisfaction, work effort and delivering optimum performance. This can be seen as an internal state of being where people feel valued and have a passion for delivering exceptional service.

The Chartered Institute of Personnel Development in the UK states there are three dimensions to employee engagement:

- Intellectual engagement – thinking hard about the job and how to do it better

- Affective engagement – feeling positively about doing a good job

- Social engagement – actively taking opportunities to discuss work-related improvements with others at work.

So what encourages employees to go the extra mile? Some say that it is a matter of recruitment and training. People who are employed with a positive attitude and high energy and have the training they need to do the job well are most likely to go the extra mile. We agree that recruiting high-octane people is important and training them well is essential, but we have seen examples of employees who displayed a customer-focused attitude and approach on day one with a company, but six months later are either cynical or withdrawn or overloaded with work and finding it difficult to deliver a great service.

Other people say that excellent service companies such as online shoe retailer Zappos in the US and John Lewis in the UK were originally created as businesses with a customer-centricity that underpins all their actions. Therefore, the argument goes, it is not possible to create a customer focus in well-established organization that did not have this remit on inception and yet need to change their organizational culture.

We believe that organizations can change and become more customer orientated. Figure 1.5 illustrates the essential four factors which in our experience in addition to recruitment and training and development, encourage high levels of employee engagement and hence customer engagement.

Figure 1.5   The Building Blocks of Engagement

In addition to recruitment, training and development, the building blocks are:

1.   Freedom and accountability: empowerment is a common factor in those businesses which are customer-centric. Take luxury hotel chain Ritz Carlton for example. or logistics company FedEx. Both these organizations give their front line staff absolute discretion to deal with customer issues and problems that arise that as they see appropriate. Both these organizations provide a large monetary allowance to each employee (over £1000 in the case of Ritz Carlton) to make it right for the customer at the employee's discretion without referral to others. It is very rare that the employee uses the full amount of money that they have available, but the fact that they have the freedom to do so without referral is empowering, at the same time as holding the employee accountable for the resolution of the customer's problem.

2.   Simplification: making it simple for employees to deal with the customer and for the customer to transact with the organization with the minimum of effort. Many organizations now measure customer effort and can show a clear correlation between how simple they make it for customers to do business with them and high levels of customer satisfaction. An example of simplicity as well as personalisation is Amazon's one click facility online. General insurance company LV= has found that a score of 2.5 out

of 10 for customer effort (e.g. low customer effort) equates to a 95 per cent customer satisfaction rating.

Simplification can be encouraged by engaging employees in identifying improvements and finding new ways of making it easier for customers to do business with you. For example, award winning international call provider Lebara actively engages its team members in ideas for improvement. Employees have developed the online help facility for customers. This not only makes it easy for customers to do business with the organization but has also saved the business money in terms of efficiencies. LV= regularly engages its teams in WOE sessions over coffee with key executives. WOE stands for 'Why On Earth', and employees are encouraged to identify unhelpful procedures and policies and come up with ideas for improvement.

3.   Prioritization: too often businesses have many competing priorities which change on a regular basis. This lack of consistency and clarity around priorities leads to lack of focus on the customer and a lack of faith from employees that the business really knows what matters. Organizations need to be consistent and clear across the business that delivering an exceptional customer experience is a key priority, year after year.

Best practice service organizations have on average three clear annual priorities. One of these may change periodically but the other two remain constant throughout the year and are linked to the customer strategy.

At Stew Leonard's food stores in the US (a who's who of an employee and customer-centric business which has had a ten-year run on the 100 Best Companies to Work for in America list) the only policy they have says: 'Rule # 1: The customer is always right. Rule #2: If the customer is wrong, see rule #1.

Founder Stew Leonard Senior introduced the policy when he was taken to task by his wife for arguing with a customer who was complaining about some eggnog that had gone sour, even though the customer was clearly in the wrong. The result of the way he handled the situation, his wife told him, was that he had lost a customer and possibly many more when the aggrieved customer told his friends and family about the incident. Their policy from then on was 'the customer is always right'. This was literally set in stone the next day when Stew Leonard drove past a monument store where they were unloading granite. He stopped, bought a large slab of granite and had a stonemason chisel the two rules of the new store policy onto the rock. 'The rock,' as it's called, serves as a touchstone for training new employees about the Stew Leonard way.

4.   Leadership: ultimately the person that most impacts and influences whether an individual is willing and committed to spending discretionary effort is the individual's line manager.

The evidence for this relates to not only our own research amongst global service companies but also from empirical studies undertaken by Gallup around engagement. The Gallup Q12 global engagement survey uses 12 questions to identify levels of employee engagement. The questions relate to employees' primary needs, such as having the right tools for the job and knowing what is expected of them at work. The others address three stages: how workers contribute to the whole and are valued; organizational fit; and personal development. The Gallup survey highlights the importance of line managers valuing and caring for employees.

If you think back to the last time that you left an organization, you'll probably find that your decision was very much influenced by your relationship with your boss. People leave managers, not companies. A productive workplace is one in which people feel trusted and safe – safe enough to experiment, to challenge, to share information, to support each other, and where the individual is prepared to give the manager and the organization the benefit of the doubt. None of this can happen if people do not feel cared about as individuals.

Relationships are the glue that holds great workplaces together.

In the following chapters you'll find much more about how leaders create the climate which builds or destroys customer-centricity. You'll learn more about your own leadership style and the actions you can take to show that delivering an exceptional service matters.

Action Points

Here is a variety of actions you can take as a result of reading this chapter and to increase your own levels of customer-centricity:

1. List the changes in the way the customer does business with your organization in the past two years which have impacted on you and your team's ability to deliver exceptional customer service.

2. Assess how well your team currently responds to customer needs, including interacting with customers using the channels that the customer wishes to use.

3. Assess where your organization is on the Push:Pull continuum in relation to customer experience.

4. On a scale of one to ten, rate how well your organization listens to its customers and responds to their needs. How can you increase this score?

5. Visit an independent review website and see what your customers are saying about your organization's customer experience. To what extent are you generating customer loyalty and trust?

6. Use the service pyramid to hold a discussion with your team on how well you are delivering the basics, generating customer satisfaction and delivering exceptional service.

7. Look at the last employee engagement scores for your business and the team that you lead. What do they tell you about the levels of your team members' discretionary effort and how well your customers are being engaged?

8. Consider measuring customer effort as well as customer satisfaction and retention.

9. There are five characteristics of an empowered customer-centric environment: recruiting for attitude, providing great training and development, giving freedom and accountability, simplifying things for the customer, and making sure customer-centricity is a

constant priority. Rate on a scale of one to ten where you stand on each.

10.   Write down your initial thoughts on where your organization can improve in terms of customer and employee engagement. Share these thoughts with a trusted colleague. You will build on these thoughts in the following chapters.

Chapter 2

Qualities and Actions of the Customer-focused Leader

In this chapter we'll look at what it takes to be a great customer leader. We'll look at why leadership is important when it comes to customer experience and distinguish between when you need to lead and when you need to manage. We'll also take a closer look at why it's important to have a clear vision around customer and employee engagement and how to create this. We'll introduce you to a customer leadership model which demonstrates the attributes and qualities of a great service leader. Finally we provide an overview of the key behaviours we have noted in successful customer leaders and we'll encourage you to rate how well you currently demonstrate these behaviours.

The 'How' of Service Leadership

As we saw in the first chapter, leaders are responsible for creating an environment where staff members feel motivated to provide a service that is engaging for their customers and colleagues. Great service leadership is a combination of *how you are* as well as *what you do*.

Let's now look at what the qualities of great service leaders are. When I say leader I am referring to anyone in a position to influence others around the quality of service they provide. The word 'leader' does not have to be in your job title. You may be customer-facing or perhaps you are in a back-office environment. Your business sector may serve consumers or perhaps you are in the business-to-business space. Irrespective of who you are or what you do, if you work in a service business, line-manage or influence others, in our terms you are a service leader.

LEADING VERSUS MANAGING

In this book we put the emphasis on service leaders, not service managers, because we believe leadership is needed to deliver a great customer experience as well as day to day management. In our experience people in positions of influence within an organization often get bogged down in maintenance and control of the status quo and management of the day to day operation. While we absolutely agree that management is important, in order to create a culture of customer focus, we believe that people need vision and passion to drive improvement for the customer and to engage employees. This means rising above the present and having a line of sight to a compelling future state. Figure 2.1 describes the differences between leading and managing. So effectively, we need both management and leadership to deliver a great customer experience.

Management	*Leadership*
Practical	Creative
Safety first	Take risks
Organised	Inspiring
Supportive	Challenging
Clarifying	Intuitive
Team oriented	Independent
Necessity driven goals	Desire driven goals
Tactical	Strategic
Controlling	Motivational
Managing today	Inspirational
Transactional	Transformational

Figure 2.1   Leading Versus Managing

Leaders Create an Inspiring Vision

One of the characteristics of a great service leader is the ability to inspire and influence followers to deliver exceptional service. Great leaders create a vision of a future state that is compelling to their followers. The vision should be short enough to be memorable. Effective visions are motivational, aspirational and challenging, inspiring employees to strive to reach a high yet attainable goal. A clear vision projects into the future, and is stable. The vision does not shift or change in the face of market trends or changes in organizational structure. The most effective visions inspire employees to set high goals and reach for these goals. For example the Walt Disney Company's vision statement is 'To make people happy'. This statement is broad, but not too broad, and represents the overall goal and global direction of the business. Low-cost carrier Southwest Airlines, which has been number one for customer satisfaction in its sector and remained profitable for over 40 years has a clear vision: 'to become the world's most loved, most flown, and most profitable airline'.

WHAT IS YOUR VISION FOR CUSTOMER EXPERIENCE?

If you have not done so already, use the following questions as prompts to help you create a vision of how your organization or the part of the organization which you can influence can become more customer-focused.

Think forward a year from now (or two or three – set your own timescale). Imagine that you have created an environment of strong customer and employee engagement. Forget the constraints of today and focus on the future. Write down, picture or verbalize your answers to the following questions thinking forward:

- Who are your external customers?

- What do our external customers say to us?

- What do our external customers think about us?

- What do our external customers feel about us?

- How do we add value to our external customers?

- Who are your internal customers?

- What do our internal customers say to us?

- What do our internal customers think about us?

- What do our internal customers feel about us?

- How do we add value to our internal customers?

- What type of people are our team members?

- What do team members say to us?

- What do team members think about us?

- What do team members feel about us?

- How do we make this a great place to work?

- Who are your competitors?

- What do our competitors say to us?

- What do our competitors think about us?

- What do our competitors feel about us?

- How do we create competitive advantage?

Once you have answered the questions, look at the recurring themes and sentiments. Craft in a few words your ambition for the future for your customers, your organization and your team. You may wish to involve your team in creating the vision and gain feedback from them to ensure this is motivational and aspirational.

Having a clear vision or ambition of where you want to be and communicating this well will mean you'll be able to better engage your team members in delivering an exceptional service.

Customer Leadership Qualities

In order to better understand how to engage your team in delivering excellent service, let's look first in more depth at how great leaders approach employee engagement.

There are two types of engagement – rational and emotional. Rational engagement moves individuals from a place of potential ignorance to a place of understanding which at most will create 'informed' employees. At a logical, rational level we can provide information to employees. For example, as an organization we may publish our service vision to employees or set out a service charter or set of service standards for customer excellence. The customer will know what these are by reading the charter or standards and the employee will be aware of what they need to do to deliver them. However, this does not guarantee that employees will be motivated to do anything with the information. Communicating information like this is important and useful, but be aware that rational information will only take you so far on the road to engagement.

Emotional engagement can move people from a place of understanding to believing in something, and to becoming advocates. This emotional engagement effects how people feel about themselves and others. It moves people to 'do' something, to take action to positively serve the customer. If I am emotionally engaged with an idea, product, service, individual or activity, I will ensure that something happens.

To emotionally engage with an individual, they need to feel that you are coming from an authentic place. The individual needs to believe deeply in what you are saying; that you want to involve them in what you are doing; that they are a valued contributor to this activity and that you demonstrate energy and enthusiasm. Author Maya Angelou once said 'People will forget what you did, people will forget what you said, but people will never forget how you made them feel.'

Be Authentic

Employees quickly see past 'corporate speak' and empty words which espouse a focus on the customer but which are not a genuinely held belief or passion. This is the key challenge of customer leaders – how does each leader, in their own authentic way, create an environment where people want to follow them and customers want to engage with their people?

John Timpson, CEO of Timpson shoe repair and key cutting business, tells how it took him about 22 years to realise that he needed to engage his people to create the type of business he wanted:

> *The simple trick is to trust every colleague who serves your customers with the authority to do it their way. Give them the freedom to do their job in the way they know best. You can't create great customer care through a set of rules. Personal service is produced by people who are allowed to use their initiative rather than following a process that tells them what to do.*

Respect for others is the foundation in building a great service leader. Respect means trusting people and interacting with them in an adult to adult way, trusting that their intention is positive. Without this engaging foundation of respect it will be difficult for your customers to experience your service in a way that will keep them as true advocates.

Humility, Connection, Care and Learning

In our research around great service leaders we have identified that in addition to respect for others, the leader also has responsibilities to ensure four other area are the focus of their attention. We have developed this in to the model shown in Figure 2.2. This reflects what is required to create a positive experience for both customers and employees.

There is a hierarchy attached to this model. As we have explained, respect is at the foundation of it. The other four elements which are key attributes of great customer leaders are humility, connection, care and learning.

Figure 2.2   Customer Leadership Qualities: Respect, Humility, Connection, Care and Learning

In the following pages we've set out definitions and examples of these four areas. Each section is followed by some tools and techniques you can use to increase your effectiveness in these areas.

HUMILITY

When we look at great service leaders we can see that they are approachable and show humility. I often think of this quality when I contrast two service leaders from different organizations with whom we have worked recently. Both were highly influential leaders in their organizations. I met one in the corporate head office where his personal assistant had already briefed me on how important the leader's time was, what I could and could not say during the meeting and what approach the leader believed was important to delivering a great customer experience. The cult of personality and power surrounded the leader and people pandered to his views and were afraid to challenge or voice differing opinions.

Contrast this with the meeting I had with a senior leader from another organization who asked me to meet him in store. He was standing at a coffee machine dispensing drinks to customers and apologizing that the coffee machine was not large enough to serve many drinks at a time. He said he would personally ensure this was fixed and at the same time he asked for feedback from customers about what else in the store could be improved.

Showing humility allows everyone around you – employee or customer – to feel good about themselves. Why? Because people realize that they do not have to impress this individual, they do not have to pretend; they will not be judged and they will be accepted for who they are – a human being! A human being is not perfect and we all have our faults. When we don't need to impress, we can really push the boundaries to realize our potential.

There are a number of ways you can demonstrate humility to others as a leader:

EXPECTING THE BEST FROM OTHERS

In their book *The Art of Possibility* Rosamond and Benjamin Zander talk about the most effective ways of releasing the potential within our people. Benjamin Zander, former conductor of the Boston Philharmonic Orchestra and latterly a teacher of music, calls this practice 'giving an A' (rather than a grade B or C!)

and it can be given to anyone – your team, your boss, your customer, your taxi driver! Zander says:

> When you give an 'A' you find yourself speaking to people not from a place of measuring how they stack up against your standards, but from a place of respect that gives them room to realize themselves. This 'A' is not an expectation to live up to, but a possibility to live into.

The only condition Zander made when awarding 'A's to his dedicated music students was that students had to write him a letter in the past tense, outlining why they got their 'A'. By positioning themselves into the future they had to describe the person they dared not believe they could become. The pressure of not having to prove they were 'A' students had gone and they allowed themselves to play music from their soul and take risks they would never otherwise have taken.

Giving an 'A' means you are sending a message that you trust the person and believe they will do the right thing for themselves and for the customer. As leaders we are often more concerned about the risk that doing the best for the customer might hold rather than the 'possibility'. In later chapters we talk about empowerment and the benefits of this approach.

Supermarket Waitrose are a great example of how they give their customers an 'A' through their 'Quick Service' facility. Here customers are responsible for 'zapping' their own shopping and checking out. Yes, of course, Waitrose build in ad hoc checking mechanisms and yes, a very, very small percentage of customers will take advantage; but the overwhelming majority will not. In fact Quick Service customers are true advocates of the brand. They use Waitrose more often because of the convenience this offers and the trust that they feel they have been given. The concept overall is well aligned to Waitrose's 'partnership' strategy: all employees of the company are 'partners' and own a stake in the business. They extend this partnering approach to their customers.

TRUSTING YOUR TEAM

At hotel chain Premier Inn, each team member is empowered to offer customers their money back if they do not have a good night's sleep. The concept of giving a money-back guarantee was originally hotly debated by senior leaders who were concerned that the company would risk losing a lot of money. However, employees had confidence in the product and were given clear guidelines about how the guarantee worked. Senior managers on a regional basis stood by the guarantee and trusted their teams to implement it wisely. The outcome was that instead of costing the business money, the guarantee has been a proven way of increasing customer satisfaction, loyalty and trust in this competitive market sector.

SAYING SORRY

Everyone, including leaders, is not perfect. We will make mistakes, we will say the wrong thing and we can do something unintentionally which will upset someone. The power of saying 'sorry' cannot be underestimated and is a great way of showing you can admit your mistakes and take responsibility for your own behaviour. The outcome of this is that the individual on the receiving end feels valued and understood and the likelihood of your relationship growing stronger is greater.

I was reminded of this when I complained to a team leader of the customer service department of a major airline recently. One leg of my flight had been cancelled without warning causing me to miss my connecting flight. The attitude of the leader to whom I spoke was 'well it is not my fault', when a simple 'I'm sorry' would have helped recover the situation.

SHOWING KINDNESS AND FORGIVENESS

One of the key attributes of a customer-focused leader is being able to step into the shoes of others. This applies both when you are dealing with customers as well as when interacting with team members. On a visit to a National Trust mansion property in the UK recently, my elderly mother and I began chatting to a member of staff who turned out to be the General Manager of the property. The General Manager could see that my mother was walking with difficulty and offered her a seat in one of the downstairs rooms. The seat looked over the gardens and had a beautiful view. The manager stayed chatting with my mother while I completed a tour of the upstairs rooms. The manager showed kindness and consideration which made a memorable impact on us and enhanced the quality of our experience.

Showing kindness with team members means helping others if they are struggling, listening to their concerns, forgiving them if they have not done what you needed. Holding a grudge takes a lot of effort: allow the person a voice so you can understand what they are struggling with and how you can help. Yes, we all lead life at a fast pace these days but this pace stops us taking stock and considering the needs of others – forgiveness creates a lot less stress than lack of tolerance. Mahatma Ghandhi once said 'The weak can never forgive. Forgiveness is the attribute of the strong.'

Consider situations recently when you could have afforded someone more tolerance or could have forgiven and moved on in a positive way. What do you want to say to those individuals in retrospect?

Being tolerant and forgiving others does not mean that you ignore the potential impact of what others have done, for example if you see a member of your team completing a process inaccurately, or someone has spoken inappropriately to a customer this should not go unnoticed. The kindest thing to do is to give them feedback so that they are able to change what they are doing and become more effective. It is about how you deal with the situation – how do you give the person feedback about the impact they have had so that they understand but do not feel ashamed?

How prepared are you to offer such positive regard for others in the belief that this will be enough for them to perform to their personal best?

Figure 2.3 is an activity you may want to complete to help you focus on showing humility to others.

	Who do I find it easy to do this with and why?	Who do I find it difficult to do this with and why?	What steps will I take to doing more of this with more people ?	What do I want to see change in my relationships as a result of doing more of this?
Expecting the best from others – giving an 'A'				
Trusting my team				

Figure 2.3   Humility Self-assessment

	Who do I find it easy to do this with and why?	Who do I find it difficult to do this with and why?	What steps will I take to doing more of this with more people ?	What do I want to see change in my relationships as a result of doing more of this?
Saying sorry				
Showing kindness and forgiveness				

Figure 2.3 *Concluded*

Connectedness

The best leaders we have met in a service environment are those who are approachable and can readily make connections with others. Connectedness is all about our ability as leaders to relate to others. 'Connectedness' requires leaders to 'step into the world' of others. This allows the leader to truly understand the customer and employees' concerns, perspectives and agendas. It means being able to genuinely listen and value those ideas and work with them. It involves being genuinely curious about others and seeking to understand their viewpoint rather than pushing your own. Great service leaders can connect to both their customers and their team members.

At Ageas Insurance managers working in the claims sector for bespoke motorcycle customers recognized that their team members knew little about their customers' needs. Together with the training team they developed an in-house bespoke motorcycle training programme, using knowledge and understanding from experienced riders and experts in the field. This involved managers and team members volunteering to take a motorcycle proficiency test so they could understand what it was like to ride a bike. The training included customers sharing their enthusiasm for their bikes as well as accident investigators and traffic police coming in to explain the most common causes of motorcycle accidents. As a result the managers and their teams were much more able to connect to the motorcycle customer, to understand their perspective and to speak their language.

Being connected requires leaders to also question and challenge – if individuals believe they have been truly listened to and their points understood and valued, they are more likely to engage in questions and challenges in the knowledge that everyone is searching for the best outcome, not an opportunity to feed their ego. The nature of the questioning and challenge will appeal to the curiosity of others and the possibilities that might surface, not the criticism that individuals can associate with the word challenge. We recently observed a team leader in a service organization effectively question a team of employees. The team members had been tasked with reducing the processing time of customer requests from ten to five days, avoiding re-work, errors and delays. The team leader challenged the team to reconsider their five-day target as from a customer's perspective, a day's turnaround was the ideal. As a result of this challenge the team identified improvements which bought the time down to less than a day.

Leaders also need to be connected to what is happening outside their organization and their own sector. Customers make judgements about the experience they receive from an organization based on other experiences they receive from organizations in a wide number of sectors. The power of social networks is obviously part of this as we have already seen.

Service leaders need to look over their own parapet and be able to see things from the customer perspective. Bringing customers in to the organization, shadowing them as well as attending external conferences and forums on customer experience are all ways of doing this. We have been delighted at the value leaders have gained from a Customer Experience Executive Forum we have been running in partnership with one of the major financial institutions. Approximately 120 leaders came together every three months to hear speakers and practitioners talk about their experiences in creating an engaging experience for their customers. They shared the mistakes they have made as well as success stories and went out of their way to visit contacts from different industries so they could learn from each other's approach to customer experience.

The following questions may help you consider what further steps you want to take in the area of connectedness:

1.   Who do you need to listen to more – customers, team members or other departments? What steps will you take to make that happen?

2.   Who do you need to spend more time with so you can 'step into their world' and appreciate their agenda?

3.   What can you do internally to encourage more questioning and challenging? How can you build an environment of curiosity?

4.   What external conferences or forums could you attend or become a member of to increase your connectedness outside your own organization?

Care

Care extends again to both the customer and the employee. The great customer leader shows that they care about getting things right for the customer. For example, I am a customer of Starbucks who in my experience usually provide a good service. The last time I visited my local branch I stood for nearly 20 minutes waiting for my coffee to arrive. The barista realised that he had forgotten to make my order and when I asked apologized and made my drink straight away. The manager of the branch had seen our interaction and as I sat down came over and personally apologised for the delay. She also handed me a service recovery voucher for a free drink next time I was in the store.

Conversely, I then visited my local garden centre where the manager I was dealing with left me mid-transaction to hurry off to greet her Regional Director. The Director walked straight pass me, the customer, and began a site visit with the manager inspecting the displays and merchandising and ignoring both me and other customers.

We soon know as a customer if the person we are dealing with cares. But as an employee how do you know when your leader genuinely cares about you? This is a question we have asked leaders over the last few years when running service leadership workshops and the answers are always the same:

- Acknowledge and notice others – e.g. saying 'Good morning, how are you? How was your weekend?'

- Learning everyone's names from your direct reports to the most junior people

- Give the person your undivided attention and maintain eye contact during conversations

- Ask other's questions and their opinions and actively listen

- Provide ongoing feedback

- Regularly compliment people both publicly and privately

- Express genuine interest in the personal life of each team member

- Spend time finding out what is important to others.

This is what leaders want with regard to caring from their leaders – it doesn't seem to matter what level in the hierarchy you direct the question to, the answers are always the same!

When you look at this list, there is nothing challenging or stretching in any of these activities. Some leaders will suggest that time is an issue but of course we all know that if we believe something is important we will find time to do it. Therefore, it would suggest that leaders do not believe that the activities above are really important to others, yet it is a universal issue – we all value these activities.

I was working with a number of different groups of managers in the cargo department of British Airways and we asked them this question about what makes a caring leader. Not only did the managers consistently agree with the areas above, they named the leaders in their department who role modelled this. One leader's name kept coming up as an example of a caring leader and I made a point of finding out the name of the manager. One lunch time, just after finishing this very session, I noticed this particular leader walk through the building. He no longer worked with the original team of people but he spotted this same group having lunch and walked straight over to them. From a distance I could see handshakes, laughter and animated discussions which lasted a couple of minutes. When he left you could tell by the people in the group's faces how much that interaction meant to them. When the group came back after lunch, the first thing they said was that they had seen Mark and they had a quick chat with him and what a great leader he was.

Mark had a choice when he saw this group of managers – he could have easily avoided them if he needed to or as he did, make a point of going up to them and engaging with them. As leaders we always have choices and if we know that spending a few minutes with others chatting about them and how they are doing can make a difference to their day and ultimately how they perform, then why would we not do it?

Here are some questions for you to consider:

- How much do you know about your customers? How much do you know about your team?

  – Do you know the name(s) of their partners and children?
  – Do you know what really matters to them?
  – Do you know what motivates each of them?
  – Do you what they like doing in their spare time?
  – Do you know what would keep them awake at night?

What occasions can you create so that you have time to get to know your people better and recognize them for the contributions they make? What, for you, would be an authentic way of showing you care for your customers and your team?

Learning

Great service leaders are tolerant of others' one-off mistakes and see them as a way to learn. At toymaker Lego, the organization has set up a 'FutureLab' aimed at inventing new products and experiences for the Lego customer. The aim of the lab is to deliberately disrupt the organization from within, rather than wait until a competitor disrupts their business. They learn as much about themselves and their customers from failure as they do from success. Their attitude is 'How could we have learnt a better way of doing things for the customer, if we had never made mistakes?' As Carl Jung said: 'Everything that irritates us about others can lead us to an understanding of ourselves.'

Within the organization, feedback is a great way of creating a learning environment, particularly if it is delivered by a leader who shows humility, connects well with people and cares about them. When we have respect for a person we are willing to hear whatever feedback they have for us because we know the intent is to help us.

One way of creating a feedback culture is to invite feedback from others on your performance, your behaviour and its impact on others. By modelling how to receive it, you will be encouraging others to do likewise.

'In the moment' feedback is what all leaders want to aim for. Being able to offer each other feedback while having a conversation or just after a meeting or an interaction with a customer shows that the culture is keen to learn and do the best they can for themselves as well as others.

Leadership Qualities Questionnaire

Let's give you an opportunity now to look at where your strengths and gaps are as an engaging leader and therefore what you need to do more of or less of to create an engaging environment for your people and customers. Below is a short diagnostic. After you have completed it, use the score sheet to identify your strengths and gaps. You can also set yourself an action plan to address any gaps you have identified.

RATING SCALE

5 – I do this all the time

4 – I do this most of the time

3 – I sometimes do this

2 – I do this now and then

1 – I never do this

Consider your team and customers when answering these questions. To what extent do you:

1.   Talk openly about weaknesses and freely admit mistakes

2.   Ask and encourage questions and challenges

3.   Show genuine concern for others

4.   Give developmental feedback to others to help them improve

5.   Show honesty and consistency in the way you are with others

6.   Step into the world of others to understand their perspective

7.   Demonstrate empathy to others when they air their concerns

8.   Invite others to give you feedback on your performance and impact

9.   Make yourself accessible and listen without judgement

10.   Communicate your ideas and thoughts in a way that excites and enthuses others

11.   Show that you listen and value what others are saying

12.   Give responsibility to others so they develop and grow

13.   Show acceptance of others irrespective of their behaviours

14.   Develop networks to keep you informed and up to date

15.   Know what is really important to your individual team members

16.   Show determination and resilience even when things do not go to plan

Transfer your scores to the score sheet in Figure 2.4, then total the columns.

Column 1	Column 2	Column 3	Column 4
Q1	Q2	Q3	Q4
Q5	Q6	Q7	Q8
Q9	Q10	Q11	Q12
Q13	Q14	Q15	Q16
TOTAL Humility	TOTAL Connection	TOTAL Care	TOTAL Learning

Figure 2.4   Score Sheet

Each column represents one of the four attributes of the great service leader:

- leaders who show humility

- leaders who care

- leaders who create connections, and

- leaders who want to learn and challenge others to learn.

COLUMN 1 IS THE SCORE FOR HUMILITY

Scores between four and eight suggest there is room for improvement in this area. It may help for you to consider when you could demonstrate these behaviours more often.

Scores between 9 and 15 suggest that you may be able to show humility with some people but not all, or you may be able to demonstrate some of these behaviours but not all. It may be helpful for you to consider who you find it most difficult to show humility to and why and how you could take a step closer to demonstrating these behaviours more consistently.

Scores between 16 and 20 suggest that others will see you as someone who is transparent and honest. This will often be demonstrated in the degree of trust that others have in you.

COLUMN 2 IS THE SCORE FOR CONNECTION

Scores between four and eight suggest there is room for improvement in this area. It may help for you to consider when you could demonstrate these behaviours more often.

Scores between 9 and 15 suggest that you may be able to form healthy connections with some people but not all or you may be able to demonstrate some of these behaviours but not all. It may be helpful for you to consider in what circumstances you find it more challenging to connect with others and how you could take a step closer to demonstrating these behaviours more consistently.

Scores between 16 and 20 suggest that others will see you as someone who is energetic, enthusiastic and passionate as well as wanting to develop a strong understanding of others.

COLUMN 3 IS THE SCORE FOR CARE

Scores between four and eight suggest there is room for improvement in this area. It may help for you to consider when you could demonstrate these behaviours more often.

Scores between 9 and 15 suggest that you may be able to demonstrate care towards some people but not all or you may be able to demonstrate some of these behaviours but not all. It may be helpful for you to consider in what circumstances you find it more challenging to show you care for others and how you could take a step closer to demonstrating these behaviours more consistently.

Scores between 16 and 20 suggest that others will see you as someone who always has time for others and shows others how much they are valued.

COLUMN 4 IS THE SCORE FOR LEARNING

Scores between four and eight suggest there is room for improvement in this area. It may help for you to consider when you could demonstrate these behaviours more often.

Scores between 9 and 15 suggest that you may be able to demonstrate learning with some people but not all or you may be able to demonstrate some of these behaviours but not all. It may be helpful for you to consider in what circumstances you find it more challenging to demonstrate these behaviours and how you could take a step closer to demonstrating these behaviours more consistently.

Scores between 16 and 20 suggest that others will see you as someone who eager to grow and develop and eager to encourage others to do the same without any fear of failure.

Based on your scores, consider the areas you would like to improve to increase your ability to become an engaging leader:

1.

2.

3.

What Does it Mean to be a Service Leader Role Model?

You may now be thinking that successful customer leadership is all about the qualities that you display and role model to others. We very much believe that the 'how' of customer leadership is very important, but we also know from experience that 'what' leaders do on a consistent basis sends very powerful messages to the team you lead. Service leadership therefore is the combined effect of how you are and what you do.

In the last part of this chapter we provide an overview of the key behaviours we have noted in successful customer leaders and we encourage you to rate how well you currently demonstrate these behaviours. You'll see that the remaining chapters provide more details of what successful leaders do in each of these categories so you'll be able to focus on those areas where you need most help and inspiration.

A role model is someone who serves as blueprint for others, whose behaviour is emulated by other people and who consistently leads by example. Role modelling is a useful means to provide continuity and maintain high standards to be passed on to others. One of the reasons that people make good role models is alignment and consistency. What role models say and what they do is congruent and they continue to demonstrate the same positive qualities and behaviours on a consistent basis. When role models lose their credibility, it is often because their words and actions contradict each other (witness many people's disillusionment with politicians).

DO WHAT I DO, NOT WHAT I SAY

Leaders throughout an organization act as role models for customer-centricity. One company we worked with developed a set of values and behaviours to encourage a customer-focused organization, particularly promoting the concept of team working across the business. But these behaviours never took root because senior managers' behaviour actively promoted a sense of rivalry and lack of cooperation.

A key to being a successful service leader is making sure you are walking the talk. Communicate with others what standards you expect, ensuring you consistently apply those standards. For example, praise behaviours you want to encourage, notice how consistent you are.

Be mindful of how you represent the customer to others; be consistent and talk positively about the importance of customer-centricity. If you are part of the management team, toe the line: do not role model disunity by talking about team members behind their backs or questioning collective decision making.

WHAT DOES IT TAKE TO BE A CUSTOMER ROLE MODEL?

Being a role model for delivering a great customer experience is all about being conscious of what you stand for, the behaviours you demonstrate and the impact these have on others.

- Self-reflection and self-awareness are important. Take a minute to consider what is really important to you: for example is it the customer, achievement, team work, fairness?

- How well aligned is this to your organization's values?

- What sort of role model is right for the organization?

- What behaviours is it important to role model?

- Next, think about what behaviour it is that you are currently modelling? How sound is this? How aligned is the behaviour with the value of customer-centricity?

- Consider your public behaviour but also your behaviour outside the public gaze.

- Assess the current impact that your role modelling is having – 360-degree feedback can be a useful tool here.

- Develop a clear view of the behaviours you currently demonstrate. Discuss and agree the impact of these with your colleagues and team.

- Identify what behaviours you project a positive role model for around the customer and others that may need adjusting or developing. The following self-assessment should help in this regard.

How Can I Tell if I am Role Modelling the Right Customer-centric Behaviours?

You cannot get engaged customers and employees without gaining insights into what is important to them, creating standards and processes that will deliver what they want, measuring how successful you have been and then continuing to innovate and redesign with the customer and employee's input and involvement.

In our experience of working with a wide number of customer-centric organizations and in researching customer leadership for this book, we have identified six key behavioural sets as shown in Figure 2.5 that effective service leaders demonstrate:

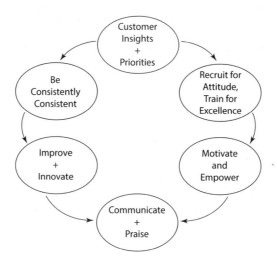

Figure 2.5   Role Model Customer-centricity

Customer Insights and Priorities

This set of behaviours involves getting close both to the internal and external customer, using customer insights and feedback to drive the direction of your team's service delivery. It also involves ensuring that the customer is a key strategic priority and that this is translated in to key performance indicators for everyone throughout the business.

Recruit for Attitude, Train for Excellence

The saying trips off the tongue, but how many service organizations truly take this approach? Effective recruitment takes time and effort and leaders should not underestimate the importance of selecting for a positive attitude and approach to the customer.

Motivate and Empower

Great service leaders create an environment where people want to give of their best. This means adopting a leadership style that both supports and challenges individuals as well as understanding what motivates each person in the team. It also means consciously empowering individuals to do what is best for the customer.

Communicatione and Praise

Whether you are in an external customer facing role or a back-office support function, you need to consider how far up the communication agenda you put your customer. Linked to communicating with and about the customer is the importance of catching people getting it right and praising those who deliver exceptional service.

Improve and Innovate

Customer expectations are constantly rising as is the way the customer interacts with businesses. In the age of digital media, how well are you keeping up with demand? What actions do you take as a leader to ensure that your customer experience is constantly improving and also that you innovate to meet as yet unseen demands?

Be Consistently Consistent

The challenge of embedding a customer-centric culture throughout an organization is to ensure that every part of the business is aligned and that the customer remains a key priority, consistently. It is widely thought that it will probably take you anywhere from two months to eight months to build a new behaviour into your life. At work, one of the challenges we see with customer experience is that the organization often has changing priorities and when one initiative has been introduced, e.g. service leadership, it is easy for this to be abandoned when another programme appears. Being consistently consistent and on message in terms of behaviours around delivering a great customer experience is essential if you want to put the customer into your DNA.

Assess Your Customer Behaviours

Use the following self-assessment in Figure 2.6 to see where your customer-focused behaviours are strong and where you may need to refocus your attention.

SCORING

5 = I always do this

4 = I nearly always do this

3 = I sometimes do this

2 = I rarely do this

1 = I never do this

Section 1: Customer Insights and Priorities	Your Score
I regularly interact directly with customers and ask them for feedback	
I track and monitor customer views and opinions of our service on a regular basis and develop service improvement actions as a result	
I review and anticipate customer trends and needs and act on these	
I make delighting the customer a key strategic priority for my team	
I have given everyone in my team a personal objective linked to delivering exceptional customer service	
Total Section 1: Customer Insights and Priorities	
Section 2: Recruit for Attitude, Train for Excellence	
When recruiting new people to my team, having the right attitude is a key priority	
During the recruitment process I am able to observe candidates in customer situations and assess their customer-focus	
I communicate and set clear expectations about the standards of service our customers expect with all team members	
I provide regular on-going training around service throughout the year to all team members	
I focus the team on delivering brilliant basics	
Total Section 2: Recruit for Attitude, Train for Excellence	
Section 3: Motivate and Empower	

Figure 2.6   Assess Your Customer Behaviours

My leadership style balances both supportive and challenging behaviours in equal measures	
I adopt effective strategies to engage the less motivated people in my team to deliver excellent service	
I empower team members to make service decisions for the benefit of the customer without referral to me	
I know what the key motivators are for each of my team members	
I actively remove the blockers to high motivation in my team	
Total Section 3: Motivate and Empower	
Section 4: Communicate Customer and Praise	
I put customer service as a key item on all team meeting agendas	
I regularly share customer feedback with all team members and encourage them to give their ideas for improvement	
I share with team members when and how service improvements will and have been actioned	
I regularly catch people getting it right and I recognise others for their effort and achievement in delivering excellent service to customers	
I regularly review, communicate and celebrate progress in creating customer advocacy	
Total Section 4: Communicate Customer and Praise	
Section 5: Improve and Innovate	
I display a passion to listen to and resolve the root cause of customer complaints	
I involve my team in generating and acting on ideas for improvement in the customer experience	
I prioritise improvements in service delivery, recognising which areas will have most positive impact on the customer	
I am aware of trends in customer experience and how to address these	
I encourage innovation and fresh thinking about how to delight the customer in the future	
Total: Section 5: Improve and Innovate	
Section 6: Be Consistently Consistent	
I observe team members in their interactions with customers and provide on-going feedback on service behaviours	
I regularly communicate and remind team members about exceptional service	
I include observations about service excellence in one to one reviews, feedback and coaching sessions	
I provide a high level of personal service to my team by being approachable, making myself available and letting them know when and how I am contactable	
I have a plan of action across the next 12 months of the behaviours I will personally display and promote to encourage exceptional levels of service	
Total: Section 6: Be Consistently Consistent	

Figure 2.6   *Concluded*

Strengths and Stretches Summary

Using the scores from the above self-assessment, identify the behavioural sets which are your strengths and where you make a good role model. Likewise, look at where you have scored the lowest and consider what you can do to improve. We hope that the following chapters will provide you inspiration on how to do this.

Chapter 3
Customer Insights and Priorities

Businesses which are customer-focused have a culture where everyone, no matter where they sit in the organization, has a clear picture of what is important to the customer and the part they play in helping deliver an exceptional service.

In this chapter we look at the role of the leader in gaining, understanding and disseminating customer insights. We also look at how service leaders can ensure that customer excellence is a strategic priority at an organization, team and individual level. We cover some tips on how you can get closer to the needs of the internal customer if you work in a back-office function too.

At the end of the chapter is a list of practical actions you can take to gain customer insights and to ensure that you make customer focus a key priority.

Getting Close to the Customer

There are few organizations that we have come across who do not include the customer as a key performance metric for their organization. There are also few organizations we have come across where debate does not ensue about the pros and cons of different ways of surveying customers. Typical methods involve measuring Customer Satisfaction, Net Promoter Score and Customer Effort Score.

Net Promoter Score (NPS) developed by Satmatrix and Fred Reichheld is globally one of the most widely used measures of customer loyalty. This asks customers to what extent on a scale of 1 to 10 they are likely to recommend the organisation. Customers who score 9 or 10 are called Promoters and are most likely to remain loyal to the organisation, to repeat purchase and to recommend. Those who score 7 and 8 are called Passives, satisfied but unenthusiastic customers who are vulnerable to competitive offerings. Customers scoring 6 or less are called Detractors and potentially spread bad news about the way the organisation has dealt with them. The Net Promoter Score is arrived at by taking the percentage of customers who are Promoters and subtracting the percentage who are Detractors. NPS is a useful benchmark for your organisation's customer loyalty. Open sources on the internet for example report 2014 NPS for Apple iPhone as +67, Amazon +64, Southwest Airlines + 62 and Zappos + 60.

Whatever the measure, the best service leaders use customer insights to recognize success and to drive change. Theme park operator Disney, for example, has invested heavily in 'guestology': understanding its guests' wants and needs and going above and beyond to deliver them. All employees at Disney are called 'the cast' and as soon as they step from backstage in to the magic kingdom they are expected to 'perform'. Mirrors are placed at exits backstage so that cast members are reminded of this. Appearance standards are set from the outset. Disney has used its guestology to define four components of a 'good show'. These are Safety, Courtesy, Show (providing a memorable experience) and Efficiency. The organization has defined a priority order for these components, with safety being of paramount importance and efficiency the fourth. This helps cast members when it comes to decision making so they know that safety always comes first.

Disney's customer insights have helped them focus on attention to detail in getting the basics right. Hotel room doors in the parks have two peep holes: one at the usual height and one at a child eye's level. Trash cans in the park are set out at regular 27-feet intervals because this is the maximum distance the park designers observed guests would carry a piece of rubbish before throwing it away. They also have a set of service standards. These are: seek out guest contact, eye contact and smile, provide immediate service recovery, preserve the magical experience, thank each and every guest. The service standards are printed on cards carried by all staff so the standards are all understood and remembered.

GET BEHIND THE METRICS

Often we find that the richness of customer feedback is lost in the measures used to gauge success. It is great for example to be able to measure Net Promoter Score or Customer Effort, but where are the pain points for the customer and the opportunities to differentiate and improve?

Delivery company FedEx monitors leading quality indicators called Service Quality Indicators (SQI) that it uses to guide management and employees' efforts. The 12 key components of SQI have been determined through extensive customer research and represent the most important service and operating dimensions correlating with customer satisfaction. Some of these include damaged packages, lost packages, missed pick-ups, aircraft delays and complaints.

The leading indicators were determined via extensive qualitative feedback with customers to find out what was really important to them. Too frequently we find that service leaders do not look behind the key performance indicators and drill down into what the metric means for their team or function. We often find that qualitative data such as verbatim comments from customers holds richer insights than the metrics along.

Likewise we find that businesses often rely on one source of customer feedback, ignoring the insights that can be gained via other sources such as social media. Amongst a range of feedback mechanisms, BMW in the UK actively encourages its customers to rate each of its retailers' for their sales and service experience on-line. They like other best practice organisations also monitor social media for other customer feedback including complaints. A report by Future Foundation showed that more than three quarters (76 per cent) of those that had complained to service providers shared their experiences and more than half of these (54 per cent) did so in an online environment. Those who were happy with the dealing of and the outcome of their complaint were also more likely to share their positive experience via social media with nearly a third (30 per cent) doing so compared to just over one in five (23 per cent) of dissatisfied complainants.

Leaders need to also create opportunities for first-hand customer feedback opportunities via face-to-face contact with customers such as focus groups and shadowing the customer as they interact with the organization. At Chiltern Railways for example, leaders hold regular 'Meet the Manager' meetings at railway stations across their franchise. There are ten meetings scheduled for example in 2015. They find them extremely useful as a '2 way' communication channel. Managers get to hear what customers really think about their services and they also have a chance to explain why they do things the way they do. Questions and responses are posted as a result on the website.

MAKE THE METRICS TALK

It's great to measure customer advocacy but how well do you communicate the insight this provides to your team and use the information to help drive improvement? Best practice is to speedily make customer insights available and also to take action as a result.

At charity The National Trust, we have been helping leaders in each mansion and countryside location to create a service improvement plan with their teams, based on visitor insights. Each team reviews the range of different visitor information that it receives from online and face-to-face surveys, comment cards, Twitter and TripAdvisor. This allows the teams to identify what is important to different customer types, how well they are performing in each function and what they need to do to improve. Teams share the insights and actions via team meetings, one-to-one reviews and notice boards.

As part of a transformation programme at another train operator, East Coast, in order to make customer feedback more accessible and individual to all employees, the customer was no longer called 'the customer' but 'Mrs Jones'. By personalizing the customer and giving her a name, employees were more able to relate to the feedback and when making decisions asked: 'What would be best for Mrs Jones?'

CUSTOMER JOURNEY MAPPING

One method that we have seen been successfully used in an increasing number of organizations is looking at the journey the customer takes in interacting with your product and service from both a rational and emotional point of view. This is based on research from the Nobel prize-winning psychologist Danny Kahneman who mapped the customer experience journey on an emotion curve. He argues that customers will remember their experiences by whatever the 'peak' in their experience was (whether high or low) and by the ending. If there was a high point at some point during the experience, and you make it a great ending, it will be remembered as an overall positive experience.

For example Scandinavian Airlines (SAS) have mapped out the customer journey and focused on the key touch points for the customer from 24 hours prior to flight to collecting their bags. Their customer insight showed that customers wanted an automated service, but wanted a person nearby if needed. So SAS provided assistance at all automated check-ins. Staff added on 'chat' to make the experience memorable. (Their customer survey showed that customers who were greeted with a friendly smile and hello easily forgot the interaction. By adding a more memorable conversation, the airline saw a significant increase in customer satisfaction scores.) To encourage conversation staff wear badges that encourage customer comment ('You had me at hello', 'Today I'm on fire!' 'Experienced and still sparkling' 'Happy hour starts now!').

By mapping out the customer experience in each part of the journey, businesses can identify effort points and minimize or eliminate them. An effort point is a point in the journey where the customer has to make too big an effort to move through that step – to such an extent that they may choose not to bother! Examples of effort points in your business might be long queues or complicated admin that the customer has to complete.

There tend to be three basic things you can focus on to reduce the effort required from the customer:

1.   Reducing the time on the task

2.   Making the transaction more convenient

3.   Making things simpler.

If effort points are not addressed they can cause dissatisfaction amongst customers which could lead to defection. Insurance company Aviva makes substantial use of customer effort minimizing techniques.. Teams visualize the customer experience and how it feels to be a customer. In some cases customers are filmed to help bring the experience to life and so that managers and staff can see the unintended consequences of their actions.

Use Customer Insights to Drive Priorities

Customer orientation cannot happen in isolation. It needs to be seen as a key strategic priority for the business. This means that leaders need to clearly communicate the organization's intent to deliver the an exceptional customer experience.

Best practice organizations have a clear road map for how they will drive the customer experience. They recognize that it is a long-term journey that needs to be sustained over time. At global engineering company Atlas Copco, its compressor division is on the fourth year of a journey to customer excellence. Being number one for customer experience in its sector is a key strategic priority. In order to achieve this goal customer care training takes place across the business on an annual basis as well as project improvement teams working cross-functionally to identify root causes of customer issues and to bring about change. Leaders in the business also communicate the importance of everyone delivering an exceptional customer experience. They set expectations that each department or team has an important part to play in delivering this ambition and provide individual and team recognition of service success. The result has been a year on year increase in both Net Promoter Score and employee engagement.

SET CUSTOMER EXCELLENCE OBJECTIVES

If you have not done so already, embedding a customer excellence objective in every person's key performance indicators is a great way of making delivering customer experience relevant to each individual. We will talk in Chapter 6 about the importance of individual recognition and praise.

The Internal Customer

Many back-office functions can feel remote from the customer and often from the front line teams that they serve. Often they have little direct contact with the end customer and they have little face-to-face contact with front-facing teams. In addition they may not share the same metrics as front line teams and this can drive different behaviours. In our experience this is characteristic of both business-to-business and business-to-consumer-type organizations. So how can internal departments become more customer-orientated?

One of the key mindset shifts is to create a culture where non-front line people believe: 'If I'm not serving the end-customer, I'm serving someone who is.' This focus on the internal customer means that every team and every department, irrespective of where they are in the organization, has a customer – the people to whom they supply a service. This is often a mindset shift for many people who may be used to viewing the people with whom they interact as stakeholders rather than customers.

Many of the approaches to how to create a culture of service excellence within front-facing teams can be applied to internal teams.

LEADERSHIP AND VISION

An internal department will not sustain long-term customer-centricity unless its leader believes and shows via their actions that delivering a great customer experience is imperative for the team. We talked in Chapter 2 about the importance of creating a vision of the customer experience the team can deliver. However, the creation of the vision or ambition should not be done in isolation. The leader needs to involve team members in meetings, discussions and focus groups around who are the team's customers and the ambition of the team in terms of customer experience. This process can help build engagement and commitment to the vision.

CUSTOMER INSIGHTS

It is essential to use customer insights as part of this process. What do the people to whom the department provides a service believe the department or team does well? What can they improve? What other or additional services do they want to see? What services do the team provide that no longer meet the customer requirements?

For example, we worked with a finance team in a business-to-business organization. As a result of the customer feedback, the team discovered that one major report which they had produced for many years on a monthly basis was not valued by their customers. Customers only looked at one section of the report and discarded the rest. Many people in the finance department were involved in collating the information for the report but no one over the years had stopped to ask if this was useful to their internal customers. The team discovered via actively asking for feedback and then holding discussions with their internal customers that there was different information required which was of more value to them. This saved time and helped the department become more efficient. It also led to higher levels of internal customer satisfaction.

Internal teams across a retail organization with whom we worked decided to seek feedback from the retail network – regional directors, area managers and branch managers – about the service provided by head office and their distribution centre. The retail network rated each internal function and gave it a score on a scale of one to ten for how well each team was providing a service that the network valued. The resulting league table and qualitative feedback spurred each team to develop an action plan for improvement. The feedback process was repeated on a six-monthly basis and has been a major driver in improving internal service quality.

One leisure business with whom we work holds customer experience workshops for all of its employees on an annual basis. As part of the intervention, everyone is asked to identify internal blockages and barriers to delivering a great customer experience. The leadership team reviews the resulting outputs and engages team members in leading and being members of project teams to address the key issues.

Last year for example eight project teams were formed on topics ranging from creating a better who's who guide for the company to improving technical support. The project teams were made up of a cross-section of roles and represent all levels of the organization. The teams identified the root causes of the issues and worked on solutions which they then presented to the executive and communicated via the company webinar updates and newsletter. As the customer experience workshops are held on an annual basis, all employees also receive an update on the improvements the project teams have made each year. They then have the opportunity of discussing ideas for further improvements to enhance the customer experience.

CUSTOMER METRICS

Another step in creating an internal customer experience culture is to be clear what standards customers expect of the team. Using internal customer feedback, leaders can help the teams identify service standards. These standards or team customer charter outline the basic levels of service that the customer will receive. They can apply to anything that is relevant to customers: turnaround time on emails, how a report should be presented, how to answer the phone etc.

The benefit of setting the standards, and doing this in a collaborative way with all of the team, is to ensure that the basics of the service the team provides are delivered consistently. It also helps when new members join the team as they are then aware of what is expected of them.

It is possible to link the standards to the organization's values or external customer promises, for example one organization we work with has a value around 'warmth'. We helped the audit team relate this to the work they did. Although the team recognized that they needed to be objective in their work, they could add a degree of 'warmth' in the way that they communicated with their colleagues, for example in the language they used in their emails and in internal communication. This shift in tone helped the department be seen as more approachable – their internal scores for helpfulness increased. We will talk more about service standards in the next chapter.

Many businesses are driven by metrics and to embed a customer-centric culture in internal departments it is helpful to have a customer-centric metric which is relevant to the department. There are a range of metrics that businesses can use such as Internal Net Promoter Scores, Internal Customer Satisfaction, Customer Effort, Customer Easy and Customer Closeness scores.

Our view is that whatever the metric it should be relevant to the department and team and that the team should be able to gain insights from the metric and take action as a result. We have found that creating team service improvement plans and monitoring and reviewing these on a regular basis drives internal service quality.

CLOSE TO THE EXTERNAL CUSTOMER

One of the barriers to creating an internal customer focus is the lack of closeness to the end customer. Team members in head offices or satellites may never interact with customers or experience the organization's products or services. Here are a number of ideas for how you can encourage internal teams to get closer to the external customer, thereby better understanding the role that they can play in delivering an excellent service:

- Back to the floor

We have all seen the television programmes where senior leaders engage in 'Back to the Floor' activities. However, we would challenge why this needs to be restricted to the upper echelons of a business. We would encourage internal teams to find opportunities for members of their teams to spend time in branches, contact centres, out on the road etc. This takes effort and planning but we have seen team's understanding of both external and internal customer needs grow as a result. The activity works best when people are tasked with then sharing the knowledge they have gained with their colleagues.

- A day in the life of

If it is not possible for everyone in a team to go back to the floor, then bringing external customers in to the building in person or via other medium such as film allows internal teams to better understand what customers want and need from the service.

We have successfully run team events where actors have replicated real-life customer experiences as well as where front-facing employees have demonstrated what it is like to be on the sharp end.

- Job swaps and secondments

A great development opportunity is also to offer job swaps between roles, for example front line and back office staff and secondments to front line teams.

People who take on these opportunities can not only enhance their careers but also bring back useful insights to the team.

- Mentoring

A further opportunity is for internal team members to become mentors of front-line colleagues who wish to make the transition into head office. There are many benefits for both the mentor and mentee from these schemes.

- Training

We've also seen shifts in attitude towards the customer occur when internal departmental team members take part in development interventions designed for front-line teams.

OPEN COMMUNICATION

The essence of these activities we have described above is to keep open communication lines going between the team and the internal customer. So for example, when marketing creates a new customer campaign, they not only communicate it first to other teams before telling the customer, but they will already have involved and engaged representatives of front-line and internal-facing teams in the development process.

Financial services organisation, Nationwide, took a real-time approach for developing an app for its external customers. The development team not only involved external customers via focus groups in its development, but invited internal team members to add their ideas and then test and review the product as it was developed.

Team members have great ideas and given the freedom and responsibility, they can invariably find better ways of delivering a great service. Internal departments often harness the power of the team in initiatives to drive efficiency. However, they often forget to look at ways in which processes can be made easier and simpler for both the internal and external customer.

Other ideas to encourage an internal customer focus are:

- Internal workshops to heighten service awareness

- Cross-functional process improvement groups

- Publicity internally and externally on who to contact about what issue

- Organizational structural redesign, including geographical and layout relocation

- Establishing a problem escalation process to resolve issues

- Encouraging employees to 'own' a problem from start to finish.

There is no silver bullet when it comes to creating an internal customer focus. Nevertheless all our work does show that the leader of a team and their leader need to demonstrate that customer focus matters.

Actions You Can Take as a Result of this Chapter

1.   Get behind the customer satisfaction KPI that relates to your part of the business: find out what is really important to your customers and what the opportunities are for improvement.

2.   Use a wide range of methods to identify and track customer insights, e.g. social media, focus groups, comment cards, questionnaires, user groups etc.

3.   Spend time with your customers: go to them or invite them in to your organization, watch and listen as they interact with your products and services, find out what they like and where your team can improve. Share your findings and involve your team.

4.   Share on a regular basis customer insights with your team. Make these readily accessible and relevant.

5.   Develop a service improvement plan with your team and monitor and add to this regularly.

6.   Undertake a customer journey mapping exercise with your customers and your team.

7.   Identify effort points – both for your customer and for the team – and set a plan of action to reduce these.

8.   Instigate innovative ways to make customer data come to life: who is your Mrs Jones?

9.   Set organizational and team priorities based on customer insights.

10.   Set everyone in your team a customer objective.

11.   Identify who are your internal customers and gain feedback from them about the customer experience you provide and how this can be improved.

12.   Use techniques such as shadowing and job swaps and joint training events to encourage internal team members to get closer to external-facing colleagues and customers.

Chapter 4

Recruiting for Attitude, Training for Excellence

In this chapter we focus on:

- The importance of having a positive attitude and high energy to serve the customer well and how you can assess this

- Tips from top service organizations around recruitment and induction techniques

- The importance of setting service standards

- Developing emotional intelligence and the importance of ongoing development for service excellence

We hope that this will help you assess how you currently hire and develop your team and the steps you can take to improve this.

The Importance of Positive Attitude

In his book *Hiring for Attitude*, author Mark Murphy says that out of the 20,000 new recruits that he tracked in organizations, 46 per cent of them failed within 18 months. When questioned about the reasons for the failure in the recruitment, 89 per cent was down to attitudinal reasons and 11 per cent due to lack of skill. The attitudinal gaps included lack of 'coachability', motivation, temperament and low levels of emotional intelligence.

In this chapter we want to explain what to do to evidence that the person you may be hiring is truly customer-focused and can display a positive attitude in terms of coachability, motivation and emotional intelligence. Former CEO of Southwest Airlines, Herb Kelleher, was one of first promoters of 'hiring for attitude'. He said 'We can change skill levels through training, but we can't change attitude.'

The reason we are looking at this area of recruiting for attitude is because of the strong link it has with creating engaged employees and engaged customers. We know that engagement comes from how the employee and customer are 'feeling', so best practice service organizations are now recruiting people using criteria based on how they will make their colleagues and customers feel.

We have used Southwest Airlines as an outstanding example of 'recruiting for attitude'. In January 2015, they reported their forty-second consecutive year of profitability. Their pre-tax return on invested capital (ROIC) was 13.1 per cent, nearly double what it was for the year before. Southwest is the only sustainably profitable airline in US. They make a point of attributing this to the efforts of their people and they know that 'recruiting for attitude' plays a huge part in ensuring that they continue to maintain their profitability.

Libby Sartain, vice president of the People Department in Southwest Airlines, says 'taking a job with Southwest is like joining a cult. The ultimate employee is someone whose devotion to customer and company amounts to a sense of mission, a sense that 'the cause' comes before their own needs.'

What Does 'Recruiting for Attitude' Mean?

In order to recruit for attitude, the organization needs to be really clear what it stands for, and what values and behaviours support that vision, otherwise it does not know what to look for. For example, Southwest Airlines has many values but it has an overriding sense of 'fun' and 'non-conformity'. That will guide them on what they need to look for. Linda Rutherford, vice president of communication and strategic outreach at Southwest Airlines supports this:

> We hire for attitude and train for skill, and even in positions that require specific skills (such as pilots), attitude continues to be a top priority. Successful candidates should embrace teamwork, demonstrate altruism, possess a self- deprecating demeanour, take their work – but not themselves – seriously, and do what is necessary to help the company reach its goals.

Ann Rhoades, executive vice president of human resources at Doubletree Hotels Corp, a hotel chain based in Phoenix USA, used to work at Southwest

Airlines and has adopted their hiring methodology into Doubletree. Rhodes describes the Doubletree culture as freedom, informality, and flexibility. Her acid-test interview question for job candidates is, 'Tell me about the last time you broke the rules.' A long silence or a noncommittal response is an indication that a candidate is trying to figure out what she wants to hear. 'The good ones,' she says, 'don't care.' She admits to recruiting a senior financial analyst who told her he never broke the rules. She convinced herself that he might change because he had very strong qualifications. It wasn't long before he resigned.

So 'recruiting for attitude' means recruiting people based on the behaviours you see and their fit with the culture of your organization.

Recruitment Techniques

Recruitment should not be based on 'gut' feel about attitude. Rather, translate the attitude you are seeking in to behaviours. Use specific criteria, based on the definitions of the desired behaviours you are looking for and score each candidate against these. Recruiters need to have a discussion about how they arrived at those scores and need to support their scores with examples.

Competency-based Interview Techniques

A widely used recruitment technique is to ask what is called competency-based questions to discover candidates' suitability for the role. For example, if one of your values is respect, you may want to define what that means in your organization and then create the measures that you are going to use when interviewing your candidate or observing them in action. Here is an illustration of how respect can be further defined as:

- Considering everyone' needs, recognizing skills, expertise and other's contribution

- Celebrating what people have achieved for each other and the business

- Never taking anyone for granted

- Understanding that all our customers are vital, regardless of contribution.

Measures that support this are:

1.   We listen and ask questions to understand our people

2.   We treat people with dignity regardless of role or position

3.   We welcome and celebrate diversity and difference

4.   We recognize expertise and excellence on a daily basis, celebrating our successes

5.   We stop what we are doing, listen and respond to everyone who walks through our door

6.   We create an empowering environment for great performance, developing, coaching and encouraging each other.

In their book *Character Strengths and Virtues* Christopher Peterson and Martin Seligman suggest that there are certain traits that are present in all successful service-orientated recruits regardless of the culture of the organization. They suggest that the four most common are Optimism, Hope, Curiosity and Zest.

How can you identify whether your candidates have these traits in abundance? Let's start by defining what you would be looking for in each of these traits – ask yourself the question – what would the person I am interviewing have to be saying and doing in order for me to believe they were optimistic?

OPTIMISM

This is about candidates demonstrating through examples and through their behaviour:

•   Confidence about the future success of something

•   A belief that there will always be a way around a problem

•   A really challenging or difficult problem allows us to learn more about ourselves and the situation.

Here are some questions to you can use at interview to identify optimism:

- Tell me about a time when you were faced with a really challenging or difficult customer situation. What was your your approach to the problem?

- Tell me about a time when you got down about something and felt there was no way through to resolution of the situation.

HOPE

This is about candidates demonstrating through examples and through their behaviour that they:

- Expect positive outcomes

- Are full of positive expectations

- Are realistic rather than overoptimistic

- Adopt a 'nothing ventured, nothing gained' approach.

Here are some questions to you can use at interview to identify hope:

- Describe a time when you just wanted to give up on what you were doing?

- Tell me about a time when being realistic helped to manage yours and others expectations.

- Give me an example of a time when you set yourself or others positive outcomes when they were not convinced they would succeed.

CURIOSITY

This is about candidates demonstrating through examples and through their behaviour that they:

- Want to know more

- Ask why until they are convinced

- Display a thirst for learning and exploring

- See value in change

- Proactively seek out new information.

Here are some questions to you can use at interview to identify curiosity:

- Tell me what you have done in the past to extend your learning about something

- How would you describe curiosity from a positive and negative perspective?

- What does curiosity mean to you?

ZEST

This is about candidates demonstrating through examples and through their behaviour that they:

- Display energy and enthusiasm that is contagious

- Show a passion to get things done

- Have a willingness to take on more

- Show self-motivation

- Show a willingness to take risks.

Questions to identify zest include:

- Tell me about a time in the past when you have engaged others with enthusiasm and the impact that had.

- Give me an example of when you showed real passion to get something done for a customer and how you went about doing it.

- Tell me about a time when you took a risk and what happened.

Strengths-based Interviewing

Competency interviews are based round the assumption that past behaviour will predict future performance. Competency interviews are known to be generally reliable, objective and consistent but techniques to answer questions well can be learnt. Competency-based interviews have been in vogue for some time now and do not necessarily allow businesses to evidence positive attitudinal traits. The responses that candidates give can be rehearsed and at best demonstrate what the candidate *can* do, not what they *like* doing. Many businesses therefore have been moving to a ' strengths-based' interview approach with the aim of finding out candidates' interests and what they are good at rather than what they are capable of doing. The theory is that by identifying your strengths and matching yourself to the role, you will enjoy it more and perform better that those who have to try hard to fill the role. Evidence shows that the candidate also finds the interview more engaging.

Professor Alex Linley of Capp defines a strength as: '*a pre-existing capacity for a particular way of behaving, thinking or feeling that is authentic and energising to the user and enables optimal functioning, development and performance*'. This is because when people use their strengths, they demonstrate 'flow', a real sense of energy and engagement.

Graduate recruiters, such as Standard Chartered, Ernst & Young, Barclays, Nestlé, Royal Mail, BAE Systems and Unilever all now use strengths-based interviews in their recruitment process. They find that this technique is more likely to uncover the candidate's preferences and how they might fit with the organization's culture and the job requirements. Responses to strength-based questions cannot be rehearsed and examples are such questions:

- Describe a successful day you have had

- What are you good at?

- What things are always left on your to-do list and not finished? (These are probably weaknesses: things you dislike doing)

- What makes you happy at work?

- What comes easily to you?

- What things give you energy?

- When did you achieve something you were really proud of?

- Do you prefer to start tasks or to finish them?

- What do you enjoy doing the least? (These are likely to be areas where you lack natural aptitude or skills.)

Spotting strengths comes from seeing the energy and enthusiasm of a candidate. The candidate is more authentic in their response. Strengths are argued to lead to higher performance than competencies and are easier to spot.

Experience Candidates in Action

Apart from creating question banks based on the attributes you want to explore with your candidate in either a competency- or a strengths-based interview, we strongly recommend you seeing the candidate in action in your working environment. How do they interact with team members and customers? What attitude do they portray? This will help you to make the best assessment of the fit of the candidate with your culture.

Asking questions in an interview is only one way of collecting evidence on how well your candidate is able to display the traits you want. Thinking about the four traits above of optimism, hope, curiosity and zest, you can put candidates in to a customer setting and see how they perform for the day, you can set candidates exercises such as a group discussion, a leadership task or a presentation to their prospective team – all great ways of gathering indicators of their natural ability to demonstrate these attributes.

It is also important that that you check out your observations with other members of the team. As subjective human beings we are capable of seeing things the way we want to see them! If you feel a strong rapport with a candidate be aware that you may get blinded by your own filtering process, i.e. you may see them differently to others. The best way of dealing with this is to make sure that others in the recruitment process have a chance to see them in action as well. The same can be true if you feel a lack of rapport with someone.

Here are three examples of how companies in different industries approach 'recruiting for attitude'.

Pret A Manger

Pret A Manger is Britain's leading sandwich chain with an enviable reputation for service. In *The Times* newspaper survey of the best companies to work for in the UK, based on employee feedback, Pret came tenth, ahead of some very well-known blue chip companies. It has over 250 stores in the UK, US and Hong Kong. A Pret Foundation Trust was set up in 1995 to help support the food runs and other charity projects; 10p from the sale of every tuna baguette, Love bar and Lemonaid drink goes towards it. The Foundation also funds an apprenticeship scheme for the homeless and ex-offenders, which gives three months of training and the promise, all being well, of a job afterwards.

Pret recruit people who are hard-working, enjoy delicious food and who have a good sense of humour. Any potential new recruit at Pret goes through the following steps: an online application, an interview, and an Experience Day where candidates work as part of the team in a shop for a whole day. This means the candidate and the organization get to check each other out. At the end of the day, each member of the team tells the manager whether they think the candidate would be a good fit at Pret and the manager tells the candidate there and then whether they have been successful. If unfortunately they have not, they'll explain why and pay the candidate for the day's work that they have done. If the candidate is successful, they will be welcomed into the team and the hours they have worked will be included in the first week's pay.

Pret's philosophy is that 'our wonderful hardworking people make all the difference. They are our heart and soul. When they care, our business is sound. If they stop caring, our business goes down the drain.' Their philosophy is to pay people as much as they can afford, rather than as little as they can get away with. They invest in, train and develop their people. All shops have trainers within their core staff. They run many courses at their Training Academy in Victoria, London and invest heavily in employees' development. This is reflected in the number of team managers who go on to be managers (72 per cent) and more. They employ many different nationalities and value the cosmopolitan feel this gives the company, twice a year they throw a massive party to which everyone at Pret is invited.

ZAPPOS

Zappos.com is an online shoe and apparel shop currently based in the US. It has 1400 employees. Since its founding in 1999, Zappos has grown to be the largest online shoe store. Founder Nick Swinmurn started Zappos in 1999 after his frustration with mall shopping convinced him that there had to be a better way to find the shoes you want in the colour you want and in the right size. Tony Hsieh came on board as CEO and propelled the company to over $1 billion in annual gross merchandise sales. The business has been recognised as one of the fastest growing retailers in the world. It is consistently a J.D. Power Customer Service Champion and scores consistently high Net Promoter Scores.

Zappos has a well-defined corporate culture with ten core values. These are:

- Deliver WOW Through Service

- Embrace and Drive Change

- Create Fun and A Little Weirdness

- Be Adventurous, Creative, and Open-Minded

- Pursue Growth and Learning

- Build Open and Honest Relationships With Communication

- Build a Positive Team and Family Spirit

- Do More With Less

- Be Passionate and Determined

- Be Humble.

A training team trains employees in each core value. Every employee hears the same message, learns the values, and learns the behaviour that is expected to live the values every day at work. Employees have developed an annual culture book which sets out and reinforces what is important to them as a company.

The hiring process at Zappos is lengthy and focuses on attitude and cultural fit. Zappos do not post specific job vacancies on line. They invite potential candidates to join an 'insider group' by connecting to current employees via social networking. People who are interested in working for Zappos provide personalized information including 'what's something weird that makes you happy?' and 'write your own headline' (essentially a professional summary). Zappos takes cultural fit seriously and hires slowly. It may be months before

Zappos approaches a potential candidate but in the meantime they will be linked to the 'insider group'.

Potential candidates will meet with many Zappos team members and normally attend some type of department or company event. This allows the employees who are not participating in interviews to meet the prospective employee informally. There can be a lengthy period of time between an initial cultural fit interview with an HR recruiter and an actual job offer. If a potential employee fails to pass the cultural fit interview (50 per cent of the weight in hiring), the application is not taken forward. Interviewers have developed five or six behavioural-based questions that illuminate a candidate's congruence with each of the Zappos core values. This approach to interviewing allows interviewers to assess a candidate's potential ability to fit within the culture.

If you are hired by Zappos, you can expect to spend your first three to four weeks manning phones in their call centre and learning how to respond to customer needs. Upon completion of their time in the call centre, Zappos employees are offered $3,000.00 to leave the company. If you haven't become a Zappos insider, committed to the goals and the culture, the company really prefers that you leave.

DAVID LLOYD LEISURE

We recently delivered a large-scale employee engagement programme with David Lloyd Leisure (DLL). They currently own 93 leisure clubs, with the majority in the UK although they also have a presence in Ireland, Holland, Belgium and Spain. Their ambition for their desired, future culture is to create an environment where members (customers) feel employees are consistently giving their personal best when interacting with them. DLL wanted to increase member retention and they knew they had to therefore increase employee and member engagement.

In preparation for the workshops that were run for leaders and all employees, DLL invested in research to identify what they now stood for and the behaviours that would support that. Interviews with members and employees about what was working and not working for them resulted in one clear vision 'Giving our best to help people be their best' and five behaviours to support that: being Enthusiastic, Engaging, Expert, Empathic, and Enabling. By living these five behaviours DLL believed their members would feel Special, Understood, and Valued which was what members were saying was missing for them.

Managers and employees went through an experiential workshop which encouraged them to work at both a rational and emotionally engaging level. The workshop moved them to a place where they understood what DLL was trying to achieve through this intervention before they were given the opportunity to engage personally with the behaviours. They completed an activity which allowed them to experience what it was like to be on the receiving end of their behaviours from both a positive and negative perspective. The convincer for them was feeling what it was like to experience positive behaviours and to notice the impact on others when the behaviour they displayed was negative.

These five behaviours were then applied to the DLL performance management process and recruitment process. The behaviours were defined further so they described the specific behaviour they wanted both employees and managers to exhibit and to be measured against.

This transformed their recruitment process – no longer were they recruiting for people who had 'done the job before', i.e. had the experience and skills of knowing how a leisure club works; they recruited people who they knew, through their behaviour, would make their members feel special, valued and understood. DLL have now recruited general managers for their clubs who have never been in the industry before – something that was not usual practice.

Apart from interviews, DLL also added role plays into the recruitment process so they could see specifically how the candidate dealt with a situation in the moment. Candidates would be put in situations where they would have to engage with other staff members to complete a task or lead a team towards an outcome so that their leadership style could be visible. At senior level, candidates were also 'vetted' by the staff members they would be managing. They would be invited into the workplace and staff members would be encouraged to ask them questions about their leadership style and their intentions for the department. The candidates would be expected to discuss with the staff what their expectations would be of them as their leader.

Train for Excellence

Once a candidate has been hired, training and development are important, not only to ensure that the new hire delivers excellent service, but also because development is a proven motivator (see also Chapter 5).

Induction is an ideal opportunity to establish customer expectations and introduce service standards. Standards of service need to be set by the customer and reflect what is important to them. For example, here is a checklist of standards that customers from a department store look for in terms of basic service:

- People greet me and smile

- All staff are recognizable (wearing uniforms) and have name badges

- People make it clear they are available to help but without imposing themselves on me

- People are warm, friendly and helpful

- People listen to understand my needs

- People are clearly knowledgeable and happy to share information as recommendations, reassurance or simply interesting information

- If I pick something up I'm given information on related items / lines

- I'm given advice on similar things / items I may not have noticed and on current offers

- People tempt me to try something I wouldn't usually do

- If I have children they are talked to and shown things that may be relevant to them

- People offer help if needed

- People talk to me openly and encourage me to talk to them

- If it's busy I still feel good – people are actively trying to help and still offer advice with a smile

- Someone checks all was good for me – if it wasn't they really do something about it

- It's clear people are alert to problems

- People thank me for visiting

APPLE

Apple has developed a set of service standards that set out how they expect every member of staff to behave. Called the 'Steps of Service', these are spelled out in the acronym APPLE:

- **A**pproach customers with a personalized warm welcome

- **P**robe politely to understand all the customer's needs

- **P**resent a solution for the customer to take home today

- **L**isten for and resolve any issues or concerns

- **E**nd with a fond farewell and an invitation to return.

Only 2 per cent of applicants get hired at Apple and they have extensive knowledge about products and the business. Apple have a policy called 'The talent weighted to the front'. This strategy encourages stores to put their most talented and quickest employees at the front line to ensure speedy and reliable service. To make sure they have happy loyal customers who trust their staff, Apple training encourages team members to 'un-sell' a product or service if it is not right for the customer and if a lower-priced or lesser-featured product will be better suited. The Apple Genius Bar is a tech support station located inside every Apple Retail Store to offer help and support for Apple products which customers can book appointments for face-to-face and online. Candidates for 'Genius' tech support staff undergo training in facilities worldwide, then are certified and regularly tested on their skills.

Using Emotional Intelligence to Serve the Customer

One area of recruitment and development which has been a focus for many businesses is emotional intelligence (EQ). This is the ability to put yourself in the customer's shoes and to see things from their perspective. This is most apparent when things go wrong, but EQ is relevant to every service act in the organization. If your organization does not recruit and train people around emotional intelligence then now is the time to start.

WHY EQ IS SO IMPORTANT

The most 'efficient' organizations are not always the most customer friendly. Research by Daniel Goleman, author of *Working with Emotional Intelligence* indicates that when it comes to lasting relationships it is more often how we are and how we relate to customers rather than specialist technical skills and ability which counts with others. Service providers who are emotionally intelligent are those who have high awareness of:

- Themselves and the range and depth of their feelings – sad, happy, depressed.

- Other people and their feelings and what signals such feelings give off.

- The impact they have on others.

- The impact other people have on them.

They are able to use this knowledge to manage the way they deal with other people and to change the impact that others have on them or that they are having on the customer.

Every front-line service employee knows that handling multiple customer queries each day puts them under pressure. It is very easy to take things personally, to become frustrated and stressed. Service providers with high emotional intelligence recognize their emotional temperatures and are able to control their effects. They take steps to proactively manage their stress levels and the way it comes out.

When handling customer calls, particularly difficult ones, the ability to empathize with the customer is key. Service providers with high levels of EQ create rapport with customers by speaking their own language, by showing an interest and relating to what the customer is feeling. In this way they form better relationships with customers which lead to more effective results and are able to defuse many difficult situations.

THE REALITY: FEW ORGANIZATIONS HAVE HIGH EQ

If a well-developed ability to empathize with the customer is clearly so important, why is it not universal in service organizations? What stops EQ being present throughout the organization? Here are some common reasons for poorly developed EQ.

MANY LEADERS ARE 'PEOPLE INSENSITIVE'

Customer leaders often reach positions of authority through their technical ability and their capacity to look dispassionately at facts and present information logically. The Myers-Briggs Type Indicator© measures this as a preference for decision making through thinking. Research suggests that more managers are higher on this scale than feeling, which are those who actively pay attention to others. A study of the relative ineffectiveness of IT managers serving their internal clients observed 'One of the more noticeable aspects is how many of them find it hard to get in touch with their feelings.' Such managers pay more attention to:

- facts rather than emotions

- logic rather than sensitivities.

This approach affects the ability to listen more to customers and to colleagues and to create and maintain rapport.

MANY SUFFER FROM OVERLOAD AND STRESS

In an era of downsizing and more for less, employees feel increasingly under pressure as layers of posts have been removed and they are working long hours. Fear can lead them to take on a 'siege mentality', afraid to delegate and closed to the views or feelings of others for fear it will be personal criticism, or lead to even more work for the individual involved.

THERE IS A DELUGE OF INFORMATION

As information availability has increased, so has the inability of managers and organizations to handle the data. This has led to the situation where warning signs of poor quality or customer dissatisfaction go unheeded.

SERVICE LEADERS FEAR OF LETTING GO

Many service leaders are reluctant to empower and are overly concerned to keep control. This leads to lack of trust, which others quickly pick up on.

SHIELDING OF IMPACT

We become shielded from the consequences of our actions. Employees of large organizations frequently do not feel the personal impact of their decisions. Email and voicemail have heightened this cocooning impact which can lead to an approach of 'it wasn't my fault'.

HOW TO INCREASE YOUR OWN EQ AND THAT OF YOUR TEAM

There are many approaches you can use as a customer leader to increase your own EQ and that of others in your team. Here is a selection of methods:

- Find ways during recruitment to check out the level of candidates EQ. For example, ask how they handled difficult customer problems. Watch for responses that indicate empathy and concern for the customer.

- Mystery shop your service: ask your team to experience the service they provide from a customer's perspective and to identify the feelings this experience generated.

- Mystery shop your competitors and encourage your team to do the same, noting how the needs of customers were met.

- Encourage your team to bring in examples of best practice in customer service and those which display EQ.

- Feed back comments from customers. Use customer research to identify how each service provider is performing.

- Monitor performance and provide ongoing coaching. Focus on 'how' the service provider relates to the customer as well as their knowledge or skills.

- Provide training on the skills needed in handling difficult customer situations. Put particular emphasis on showing genuine empathy to the customer when things go wrong. Studies show that complaining customers will not listen until you show that you truly understand their situation.

- Engender a 'can-do' attitude in your team by empowering them to make decisions to help the customer.

- Coach your team in use of rapport-building techniques such as recognizing customer moods and adapting service style to match, use of mirroring verbal and non-verbal cues (where appropriate), showing a genuine interest in the customer.

- Talk with your team about how to deal with difficult customer issues. Pass on this information to other parts of the organization so that steps can be taken to avoid these problems.

- Give feedback to your team on how they are performing – motivational feedback will develop their level of confidence and developmental feedback will help them to improve. Be prepared to listen to feedback on your own performance.

- Talk about what causes your team stress as part of your regular team meetings. Take steps to overcome causes of stress. Provide training to your team in stress management.

- Make time to find out the expectations of other groups and colleagues. Encourage an internal customer approach to handling their expectations.

- Acknowledge what individuals in your team are feeling and offer them help and support.

Assess your own EQ

Look at the following statements and, using the scoring system where:

- Agree strongly Score 5

- Agree to some extent Score 4

- Neither agree or disagree Score 3

- Disagree somewhat Score 2

• Disagree strongly Score 1

Rate to what extent you agree that you:

Self-awareness   **Score**

1. I am aware of situations which cause me to think negatively

2. I recognize the emotions I feel when dealing with customers

3. I recognize what influences my way of thinking

4. I know when I am angry or sad

5. I know when I feel motivated and when I do not

6. I am confident in who I am

Total score: Self-awareness

Awareness of own impact on others   **Score**

7. I know when I am not handling a customer situation well

8. I am aware of how my mood affects others around me

9. I have an accurate assessment of myself

10. I have received feedback from customers on the impact of my behaviours

11. I am aware when I make other people feel good about themselves

12. I know when my message is not clear to the customer

Total score: Awareness of own impact on others

Awareness of others' emotions   **Score**

13. I can identify customers' emotion from their tone of voice

14. I am aware when customers are upset

15. I am able to put myself in the customers' shoes and acknowledge their feelings

16. I know when someone is not being sincere

17. I can understand when customers get angry

18. I notice when others say things that are inconsistent with what they appear to be feeling

Total score: Awareness of others' emotions

Awareness of the impact of others' emotions on self   **Score**

19. I know what phrases customers use which upset me

20. I am aware when customers are trying to manipulate me

21. I know which customers I sympathize with

22. I know when someone is trying to get me to agree with them

23. I recognize when customers make me angry

24. I am aware when customers make me feel patronised

Total score: Awareness of the impact of others' emotions on self

Ability to manage self   **Score**

25. I know how to control my emotions when customers get angry

26. I am able to say no to the customer without feeling guilty

27. I am diplomatic

28. I express what I am feeling in an appropriate manner

29. I rarely take customer comments personally

30. I can change my approach with a customer if my first attempt is not successful

Total score: Ability to manage self

Analysing your Scores

Look at the scores for each of the five sections above:

1.   Self-awareness

2.   Awareness of own impact on others

3.   Awareness of others emotions

4.   Awareness of the impact of others emotions on self

5.   Ability to manage self

You need to score over 24 out of 30 in all five sections to be considered effective in creating and maintaining effective relationships. Look at the areas where you have low scores and consider the actions you can take to increase these scores.

Ongoing Development

As we mentioned earlier, one of the characteristic qualities of great customer leaders is their passion for learning. In today's digital environment, development no longer needs to be 100 per cent face-to-face although we do see value in one-to-one and one-to-group interventions. Great service organizations use a variety of learning opportunities and mediums to encourage development. The key is that learning is ongoing, focused on the customer and the culture of the organization as well as skills.

No one approach is right for every organization, but businesses who do well give time on an ongoing basis to development. One mistake that we hope you avoid is restricting service training to front line employees. In our experience while this is important, the key is to engage and train leaders throughout the business to be customer-focused. In our opinion, as this book demonstrates, customer experience is a leadership issue and customer leaders need to have opportunities to develop their leadership skills to better serve their teams and the customer.

Here are some corporate examples illustrating different approaches to reinforcing the service message.

FIRST DIRECT

First Direct (styled as **first direct**) is a telephone and Internet-based retail bank in the UK, a division of HSBC Bank plc. First Direct has headquarters in Leeds and has 1.16 million customers, 950,000 of them use Internet banking. The bank employs 3,200 people and 44 per cent of First Direct sales are via e-channels. It handles around 135,000 telephone calls every week.

First Direct has scored exceptionally well in most customer satisfaction surveys and is recognized globally as one of the best providers of customer services in the financial services sector across the world: 96 per cent of customers would recommend First Direct and one out of three new customers is via referral.

First Direct aims for a 'magical rapport' with their customers – picking up body language over the phone and reacting accordingly. There are no scripts in the call centre: 'You can see through a script. What we are asking is for people to be themselves.' There are also no 'average call handing time' targets. Customers are not passed from one person to another. The same customer representative will phone to deal with an issue.

First Direct's primary concern is to recruit the right people. They target people with good communication skills because they figure that they can teach banking and keyboard skills but not how to be a nice person. First Direct aims to be a destination employer. It wants its people to remain with the bank long term so that they can use their long-term experience to provide a better service.

After appointment, new staff undergo six weeks of training (or nine weeks part time) with 65 per cent of the time in a classroom environment and 35 per cent integrating with dedicated coaches in the live working environment taking live calls. In the first few days of training the new staff engage with the culture of the business. They then have a pattern of ongoing training and coaching to help deliver the brand's service values.

FORD

Ford is the second-largest US-based automaker and the fifth-largest in the world. In the UK Ford offered formal accreditation in customer service for all employees in its dealerships in the UK. Employees could attain accreditation following an in-depth assessment as part of the company's 'Moments of Truth' customer service initiative. This was a training investment aimed at helping Ford Retail to deliver the best service experiences to customers throughout the industry. Moments of Truth involved all 3,000 Ford Retail staff in 74 UK locations working to achieve a formal qualification in customer service.

The programme involved every employee attending a launch event and on-site workshops and working towards an NVQ qualification or equivalent in customer service. This was the first industry initiative of its kind on this scale; members of the Ford Retail board and senior management team also completed the training themselves.

Everyone worked through a series of exercises to understand what it means to deliver excellent customer service and how they can provide it themselves in their own areas. The Ford Retail view is that a 'Moment of Truth' occurs every time an employee has contact with a customer, from a salesman at the point of sale to a technician ensuring a vehicle is clean following a service.

JOHN LEWIS

The John Lewis Partnership is famous for its excellent customer service and good value ('never knowingly undersold'). It is a winner of national customer service awards for ten years running. Three out of four customers recommend John Lewis to others.

John Lewis is the largest departmental store group by turnover in the UK, with 28 stores and 4 home stores. It is the second largest privately held company in the UK. None of the 27,000 people who work at John Lewis is an employee – they're all 'partners' who jointly own the business. They get a profit share based on how much profit is generated by the business as a whole, so they all feel really involved and incentivized. This encourages them to give great service because they feel such a sense of ownership for the business. The partnership scheme makes them feel valued. As MD Andy Street says: 'We're based on the notion that if we treat our partners well, it will lead to good customer service.'

John Lewis's six founding principles of customer service are 'Be honest; give respect; recognize others; show enterprise; work together; achieve more.' New members of staff at John Lewis are sent all on customer service training days. After that, there's ongoing training for employees to make sure everyone's giving the same exceptional service. The knowledge and expertise of John Lewis's in-store staff is one of the business' strongest selling points. 'If you don't know your stuff, customers can see straight through it.' This fosters a sense of authority and trustworthiness.

Leaders at John Lewis regularly speak to front-line staff and get them involved in improving the way things are done. The philosophy is 'Front-line staff have insights no one else can form.' Partners regularly ask customers what they want and what they think, and record results. Then, they act on it. 'It's tempting to feel that once the information has been gathered, the job is done but your processes and culture need to be altered as a result', says Andy Street.

RITZ CARLTON HOTELS

The Ritz-Carlton Hotel Company operates five-star resorts and luxury hotels worldwide an independently operated division of Marriott International. The hotel chain was established in 1983 with the purchase of The Ritz-Carlton, Boston and the rights to the name Ritz-Carlton. The management company has grown from 1 hotel to 79 hotels worldwide. Ritz Carlton has 38,000 employees. The first Ritz-Carlton in Boston set the standards of service, dining and facilities as a benchmark for all Ritz-Carlton hotels and resorts worldwide. President and COO Horst Schulze's strong conviction of customer loyalty and emphasis on a value/mission-driven philosophy is summed up in the statement 'We are ladies and gentlemen serving ladies and gentlemen'.

It's consistently high standards of service are achieved by a thorough induction programme. There is a six-hour follow-up to orientation, termed Day 21, which takes place about three weeks after the new employee's start date. The General Manager conducts the first hour, soliciting feedback about the new employee's experience to date. The GM asks, 'How is it going? What did we miss? Are there issues we need to discuss or explain?'

Top performers in each of the hotel's 35 departments are drafted to be coaches/trainers in their areas of expertise. The Ritz-Carlton Line-up is the system-wide 15-minute gathering of employees every morning in their departments. The Line-up schedule is standard throughout the company; five minutes discussing what is happening at the corporate level, another five minutes talking about their hotel events and gatherings of the day and week and important guests arriving, and finally five minutes reviewing one of the *Gold Standards 20 Basics*. The Line-up is the company's most important tool in maintaining their superior service standards.

Each Ritz-Carlton employee has a card containing the twenty 'basics' and the mantra 'we are ladies and gentlemen serving ladies and gentlemen'.

Assess Your Approach to Recruitment, Induction and Service Development

Use the checklist in Figure 4.1 to assess what you do well in terms of recruiting for attitude and training for excellence.

Characteristic	In place	Needs attention
Our approach to recruitment is to hire for attitude, train for excellence		
We include measures to assess attitude as part of the recruitment process		
The hiring process includes practical assessment of candidates in action		
We consult customers and / or team members about potential new hires		
Our induction process focuses on customer service and culture fit		
We have set service standards based on customer expectations		
Emotional intelligence is part of our induction and training programme		
We train new and existing employees in customer service standards		
We provide service leadership training to managers		
Each employee has a development plan		
We provide on-going training and development to all employees		
Delivering a great customer experience is embedded in all our development interventions		

Figure 4.1   Assess Your Approach to Recruitment, Induction and Service Development

If any of the above are not in place and need addressing, consider what you need to achieve and who you need to influence to make the changes needed in this important area. Develop a plan of action for improvement.

Chapter 5

Motivating and Empowering Your People

In this chapter we look at what it takes to create an environment where people want to give of their best. We look at leadership style and its impact at work. We also discuss what it takes to empower others to take effective decisions on behalf of the customer and at the individual motivators team members need to have satisfied to become truly engaged as well as the action you can take as a leader to better understand your people.

Like other chapters, you'll find a variety of best practice examples and self-assessment tools and action plans to help you relate the key learning points from this chapter to your work environment.

High Energy and Positive Attitude

Have you ever wondered why sometimes people are not performing to their full potential or are reluctant to deliver a great service – even when you've trained them and tried to understand where they are coming from and what the issues are? Our normal reaction is to look at their levels of skills and knowledge and how to bridge the gap. However, just as important are team members' behaviours. As we have described earlier, highly engaged team members have a positive attitude and high energy and drive to do their best for the customer.

Customers can tell within seconds whether they are dealing with a committed, engaged employee or one who is fundamentally dissatisfied. This is why leaders need to be able to identify exactly what they need to do to create an empowering environment for their team.

Use the Energy and Attitude model in Figure 5.1 to help you think about where individuals in your team are most of the time in terms of their levels of engagement.

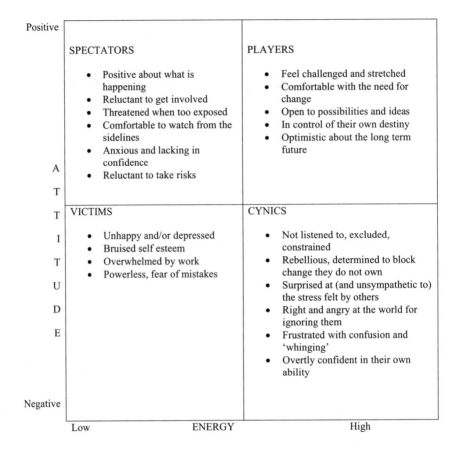

Figure 5.1   Energy and Attitude Model

This model is useful on a one-to-one basis when tackling individual performance issues. Here is how you can identify each type and the coaching opportunities they present:

- Spectators: positive attitude, low energy. *Spectators*:

  - Acknowledge good ideas but are reluctant to change themselves
  - Avoid taking risks and keep a low profile
  - Try to ride things out until things return to normal

- Spectators' coaching needs:

  - Not over-promise when they can't deliver
  - If they cannot meet deadlines, enlist other's help

  – Talk to their manager about what support they can give
  – Be more confident in putting forward and acting on ideas

- Cynics: negative attitude, high energy. *Cynics*:

  – Express frustration over pain and hesitancy of others
  – Argue against changes
  – Always see the negatives
  – Press for quick solutions and decisive actions – then criticise them
  – Are oblivious to the consequences of their negativity

- Cynics' coaching needs:

  – Talk less and listen more
  – Be aware of the negative impact they create
  – Voice their concerns in a more positive manner and criticise less
  – Ask to take on challenges and make the most of them

- Victims: negative attitude, low energy. *Victims*:

  – Block out challenges
  – Avoid confronting issues
  – Retreat into `safety' – burying their heads in the sand
  – Avoid risk, doing the minimum
  – Avoid thinking about what might happen

- Victims' coaching needs:

  – Be more confident in themselves
  – Ask for help if the task is too daunting
  – Consider the impact they are having on others, play a more positive role in the team
  – Consider what work they would really like to be doing, and do it

- Players: positive attitude, high energy. *Players*:

  – See the silver lining hidden beneath the dark clouds
  – View ambiguity and change as challenge and opportunity
  – Find humour in difficult situations and use it as a tool
  – Treat life as a continuous learning experience
  – Expand their personal comfort zone

- Players' coaching needs:

  - Set a positive example for others
  - Put forward ideas for improvement
  - Encourage and support their fellow team members
  - Tell cynics, spectators and victims when they are having a negative impact.

Support and Challenge

So how does the leader impact team members' energy and attitude? In earlier chapters we've touched on the impact the leader has in engaging their team members via their behaviours. A 2013 Gallup State of the Workplace Report, *The Relationship Between Engagement at Work and Organizational Outcomes*, states:

> *Gallup's research has found that managers are primarily responsible for their employees' engagement levels. Organizations should coach managers to take an active role in building engagement plans with their employees, hold managers accountable, track their progress, and ensure they continuously focus on emotionally engaging their employees.*

When we look at great service leaders who inspire and motivate their followers to deliver an exceptional service, we see they display a mixture of both supportive and challenging behaviours.

By supportive behaviours we mean offering motivational feedback, listening, empathizing, assisting, providing advice, guidance and back up for others, actively helping with resources via their own time and effort.

Examples of challenging behaviours are offering developmental feedback, challenging others to do better both by the requests you make of them and the stretches you set, questioning people so they rethink their actions and decisions, providing stretching goals, offering alternatives and confronting assertively.

The combination of support and challenge behaviours that the leader displays has a direct impact on the behaviour and motivation of the team as Figure 5.2 illustrates.

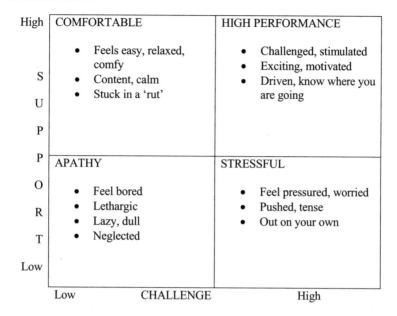

Figure 5.2 **Impact on the Team of Different Degrees of Support and Challenge**

We hope you can see a relationship between the impact of support and challenge leadership behaviours and the energy and attitude followers display.

The right levels of support and challenge will really help drive an environment of service excellence: people are supported and congratulated when they display customer-orientated behaviours and are challenged when they are seen to be displaying behaviours counter to this. They demonstrate player behaviour: high levels of energy and a positive attitude.

LEADERSHIP STYLES

The degree to which you display both supportive and challenging behaviour indicates your preferred leadership style.

HIGH SUPPORT, LOW CHALLENGE = NURTURER STYLE

Here team members are not being challenged to work outside their comfort zones and as a result they may be coasting and not delivering to the level you need them to (Spectator behaviours).

In the long term this behaviour will lead to people with talent and energy being demotivated and others believing they have permission not to deliver. To increase your challenge you make clear your expectations and provide feedback both when expectations have been met and when they have not.

HIGH CHALLENGE, LOW SUPPORT = TASK MASTER STYLE

Using this style, team members feel under pressure and may show signs of stress. They will not be performing to their optimum because of this and there will be a fundamental lack of respect for their leader (Cynic behaviour).

The task master is perceived as someone who cares little for their team and who is overly focused on tasks and results. To increase your support, you will need to spend time understanding each of your team members and their needs.

LOW SUPPORT, LOW CHALLENGE = ABDICATOR STYLE

Team members feel abandoned and may adopt a victim-like approach. The high performers will 'get on and do' but may well be expanding energy in the wrong direction which will lead eventually to disillusionment. Team members who need more direction and attention will lose motivation and self- belief quickly. Abdication is different from delegation. Delegation means you provide high levels of support and challenge.

HIGH SUPPORT, HIGH CHALLENGE = COACH STYLE

By adopting this style team members feel motivated, inspired, stretched and developed. They become players and go the extra mile to deliver for the customer and for the organization. Team members are treated as individuals and involved and consulted on their areas of expertise. This results in high performing teams.

Leadership: the Support and Challenge Model

HIGH	High Support Low Challenge NURTURER	High Support High Challenge COACH
S U P P O R T	Low Support Low Challenge ABDICATOR	Low Support High Challenge TASK MASTER
LOW	LOW	HIGH

CHALLENGE

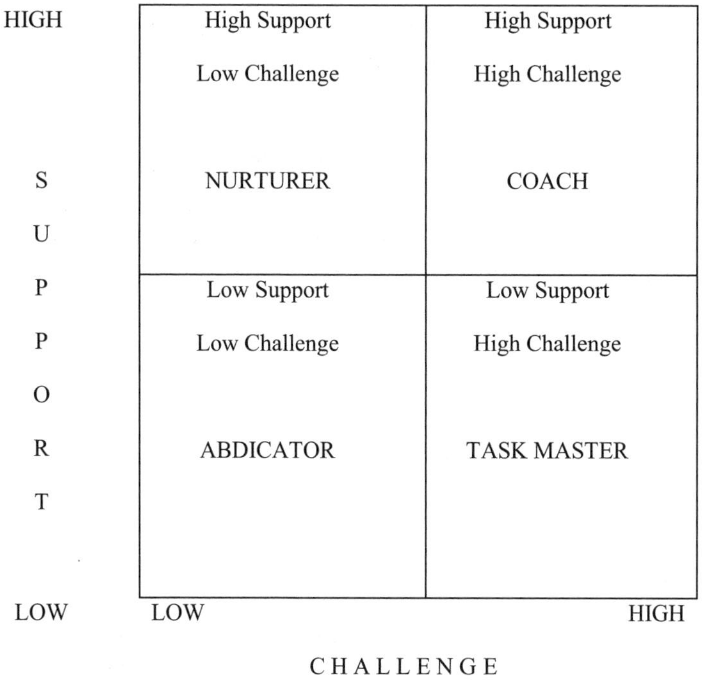

Figure 5.3   Support and Challenge Model

Use the Support and Challenge Model in Figure 5.3 to help you identify your own levels of support and challenge and the implications of that on your team members.

Consider where you are most of the time on the model and where you go when you are under pressure or stress. Next think about the long-term impact of this style on your followers and how this impacts their energy and attitude. You may need to balance your support with more challenge or vice versa in order to remain in 'Coach' mode to create high performance. Providing effective feedback is a useful leadership skill to drive player behaviour.

Feedback Skills

Part of creating a high performance climate is the continuous giving and receiving of feedback – let's face it, if we don't know how we are doing how can we look to improve?

Fundamental to being able to give effective feedback is the belief that feedback is a helpful, healthy and positive communication between two people. The purpose of feedback is to maintain and improve performance – it therefore should have both a positive intention and impact. Consequently it is vital that the whole feedback process, whether giving motivational feedback (what has gone well) or developmental feedback (where the individual can improve) is conducted in a positive and constructive way.

Here is a quick reminder of the principles of feedback and how to give it in an effective manner:

- Remember, feedback is to recognize strengths and improve performance, to keep people on track. Providing feedback on performance should be a regular part of everyone's role.

- Balance your feedback: motivational – what went well, which builds confidence; developmental – what could have been done differently, which builds competence.

GIVING FEEDBACK, SUGGESTIONS

- Be specific, use examples

- Focus on observed behaviour, describe what you see and hear

- Time your feedback, providing it when it is likely to be most effective

- Give motivational feedback before developmental, ensuring an appropriate balance between 'support and challenge'

- Avoid 'buts' and 'howevers' linking motivational and developmental feedback as the motivational praise becomes lost i.e. 'the opening was good but the middle and end were terrible'. Likewise, do not sandwich developmental feedback between two pieces of motivational feedback. This can create confusion for the receiver.

- Prioritize your feedback, recognize people's limits.

Giving effective, motivational (i.e. what went well) or developmental (i.e. what needs to change) feedback has three steps:

1.   Describe what you saw or heard someone do with no judgement:

Motivational: 'I heard you apologize to the customer for missing their agreed delivery slot.'

Developmental: 'I heard you talk over the customer when she was explaining the situation.'

2.   Describe the impact it had on the task, customer or how it made you feel:

Motivational: 'The impact was that the customer stopped shouting and allowed you to suggest a resolution.'

Developmental: 'The impact was that the customer started shouting threatening to close her account.'

3.   Describe what you would like them to continue to do or change:

Motivational: 'I would encourage you to continue to apologize, as you did, when you know that we have not delivered for the customer.'

Developmental: 'I would encourage you to wait for the customer to finish what they are saying and to then apologize if we have failed to deliver for her.'

DEALING WITH REACTIONS TO FEEDBACK

In delivering feedback, the giver needs to be conscious of the reactions of the receiver. Ideally people should be receptive to feedback and see it as helpful. When receiving feedback the individual has a choice whether to accept what they are told. However, in order to ensure that they understand the feedback, they need to listen and avoid rejecting what has been said, arguing or being defensive. Asking questions to fully clarify and seeking examples is useful. The receiver of the feedback should also ideally acknowledge the giver and show their appreciation; the feedback may not have been easy to give.

In reality a wide variety of reactions often occur. People may:

- Deny what has happened. This reaction often accompanies the initial shock of feedback.

- Show emotion. Be upset, angry or go quiet as the message sinks in.

- Justify their actions and find excuses for their behaviour.

These reactions can occur when given motivational feedback as well as developmental, e.g. ' I like your briefcase.' 'Oh, this old thing' (blushes) 'I got it cheap in a sale'.

A manager giving feedback needs to be aware of potential reactions and take appropriate courses of action to help people accept feedback. Some tips are if the recipient is in denial: reiterate the facts, what you saw or heard. If the recipient shows emotion: listen actively, empathize. You may need to postpone any further discussion until later. If the recipient of the feedback goes into justification: refer the individual to the standards expected of them, and ask them what they could do differently to prevent the situation happening again.

Empowerment

As we have seen in earlier chapters, the top driver for motivating and engaging employees is a positive relationship with the manager.

Empowerment is an important motivator for team members as well as benefitting the customer as decisions are made most speedily. The case for creating an empowering culture has been made many times. Harris Interactive, Customer Experience Impact Report 2014 found that the most successful companies are those who have leaders who not only buy into, but actively drive a customer-centric environment. Employee engagement, which we talked about in Chapter 1, is a critical factor in providing a culture where people want to work and exercise discretionary effort. Values such as empowerment and motivation cannot be given to employees or made mandatory on signing a contract but creating an environment that has a high propensity towards meeting these needs is possible.

So why is create an empowering climate the answer to engaging our people?

'Climate drives performance because it is tied directly to motivation – that is the energy people put into their work' (*Leadership & Organizational Climate*). Empowerment is created by a number of factors – company systems and policies, external factors, the politics of the organization, company strategy, having the right skills and training and what leaders do. It is estimated that 70 per cent of climate is dictated by what leaders do.

So why is creating an empowering climate so difficult in a customer service environment?

The mindset and approach of leaders will clearly impact on the degree to which the team are empowered. It is useful to look at empowerment on different levels.

LEVEL 1 – NO GO

This is where team members are not empowered, they follow and stick to the rules they have been given. No questions are asked and no action is taken unless they are instructed to do so. This is often the approach that is taken in a highly regulated environment, however that does not mean it has to be that way as the second level of empowerment may well work more effectively.

LEVEL 2 – CHECK THEN GO

This is where team members are encouraged to talk through and check the approach they are going to take to the situation with their manager before taking it.

LEVEL 3 – GO

This is where people are truly empowered to do what is best for the customer, without asking.

Consider each of the three levels and the degree to which your team members operate at each. We have found that if you want to get to a 'go' state where your team do make customer-focused decisions without referral, it is not as easy as telling team members: 'you are empowered!' Even when you give the green light and say that people can 'go' and be empowered, there are many barriers to empowerment, e.g.

- Not recruiting the right people for the role

- Not giving people the right resources

- Not training them well to give them the confidence and the skills to do their job

- Service providers seeing the same complaints happen time after time without any improvements taking place.

FEDEX

One organization that takes empowerment very seriously and reaps business benefits is logistics company FedEx. It has more than 300,000 team members worldwide. Its service area covers more than 220 countries and territories. It deals with over 6.5 million package tracking requests daily and works out of 1,173 stations, 10 air express hubs, 33 ground hubs and over 500 pick-up/delivery terminals.

The FedEx philosophy is people-service-profit. It has integrated a number of company-wide policies to align its staff with its philosophy and has a clear goal to have people who are committed, motivated and well trained.

To ensure sufficient action is taken to fix any problems, Federal Express's Customer Satisfaction Policy states that staff should: 'Take any step to solve customer problems, arrange the most expeditious delivery, provide prompt refund or credits when FedEx fails the customer.' Reinforcing this, FedEx has clearly established reimbursement and empowerment standards for different job levels and functions. These enable phone representatives to refund up to $250 without prior approval and supervisors to refund up to $10,000 over the phone. The $250 limit is based on an analysis of the average cost of handling and settling complaints and compensation claims.

FedEx will refund even when they did everything right. Along with a refund, however, the customer will receive an explanation of how the process should work and the event will be logged for reference should it happen again with that customer. Management information is used twice weekly for review to track causes and instigate remedial action. The cardinal sin is for a representative to let a customer off the phone who is not satisfied. Reps will always ask the customer directly if they are satisfied. The aim for is 99 per cent satisfaction.

BA

BA has run a wide number of service initiatives over the years. The latest, 'To Fly To Serve' promotes four behaviours for all staff:

1.   Find solutions

2.   Look the part

3.   Keep promises

4.   Do things properly

In BA's Manchester contact centre environment, the centre manager asked his team of 160 staff to say how they wanted to personalize these behaviours to fit their contact centre. 'Look the part' was less relevant for them so they focused on 'sound the part'. A training course was developed to help with tonality called the 'BA way with words', which has been rolled out to all contact centre staff.

Agents have no scripts (other than a standard call greeting) and no time limits to the calls. When they join, each new recruit is given a nine-month critical path which shows the support and development they will get. Team leaders use call replays to coach and develop their teams on a regular basis.

BA contact centres have focused on empowerment as a means of improving the service they provide. In the Manchester contact centre the team had been very process-driven and training had been built around how to say 'no' in a customer-friendly way, which wasn't going down well with staff or customers.

To help staff use their own judgement the Contact Centre Manager set up an email address called 'Find Solutions' and authorized all his team leaders to use their judgement to do the right thing.

For example, where a customer had made an innocent mistake and booked a non-refundable flight to the wrong airport, team members could authorize the amendment without charging for a new ticket. The team member then emails the details of the case to the 'Find Solutions' email address.

The centre manager runs monthly reviews with the team leaders where they discuss the different cases logged, partly to debate if this was the right thing to do, but also to check trends and see if they should challenge any of the central rules. This idea has been a great success with staff and customers and has been rolled out globally across all the BA contact centres.

Build an Empowering Culture

Let's now look at what you can do to build an empowering culture.

Look at the statements in Figure 5.4. For each action, give yourself a rating using a traffic light system of red, amber and green. Where your score is red or amber, consider the actions you can take to bring the score into a green.

To be empowered is a choice the employee makes and it takes courage to stand up for the customer in a world of conformity. Empowerment is not just about how an employee is trained or what they think about their organization – it is what they feel about their job and their customers too.

Tom Rath and Donald Clifton in their book *How Full is your Bucket?* say that everyone has an invisible bucket. We are at our best and more likely to be empowered when our buckets are overflowing. The number one reason people don't take responsibility, become disengaged and eventually leave their jobs is when their bucket is empty and they don't feel appreciated. His studies showed that 65 per cent of people received no recognition in the workplace in 2013. Teams with positive to negative ratios of three to one are significantly more customer focused and productive. So ladle the positives when you see your team members taking initiative to serve the customer. We'll talk more about this in the next chapter.

	Rating (Red, Amber, Green)	Action
CLEAR DIRECTION • I set clear performance goals and am able to link the output of the team to the direction and strategy of the business. • I state my expectations very clearly so that team members know what is expected of them and what the consequences are for delivery and non-delivery of goals for themselves, their teams and the customer		
STANDARDS • Not only do my team members know what they are being measured against but also the standard they are expected to meet. • I ensure that my team members receive training to do their jobs well • I provide feedback and coaching to help team members meet the standards expected of them.		
ACCOUNTABILITY • I encourage people to use their initiative to resolve issues, allow them to come up with ideas they believe will benefit the business and at the same time, allow them to make mistakes so they can to learn		
KNOW YOUR PEOPLE • I know what drives my team members and their individual motivators.		
TEAMWORK • I set team goals and reward the team when they have collaborated to get successful outcomes • I encourage cross functional working to positively deliver a joined up service for the customer.		
TRUST • I trust my people and they trust me in return • I listen to employees and understand their concerns, show empathy towards them when they are struggling • I do what I say I will do, admit my mistakes and show I have learned from them • I encourage and enable the team to offer suggestions and ideas for improvement • I publicise the ideas that have been carried forward and		

Figure 5.4   **Building an Empowering Culture**

Motivation

Understanding each of your team member's motivational drivers is also an effective way of 'ladling on the positives'. Dean Spitzer, author of *Super-Motivation* opens his book with some alarming statistics impacting the customer experience. In the surveys he completed for his book he reports that 69 per cent of managers said that lack of employee motivation was the most important issue for their organization. He went on to report that 84 per cent of employees said they could perform significantly better if they wanted to and 50 per cent of employees said they were putting only enough effort into their work to hold on to their jobs! The impact of these results has alarming consequences for the experience the customer will receive.

No one can motivate us to give our best: pay and conditions are important and if comparatively they are poor, this does not encourage us to give of our best. However, our motivation comes from within and it is only when our motivational drivers are being 'fed' will we feel we want to give of our best. We have encountered many service providers in poor paying jobs who still go out of their way to deliver 'above and beyond'.

We may well argue that we can be incentivized, i.e. I will give you an extra £500 if you can work two hours later this evening. But let's be clear that incentivization is very different from motivation. Many sales people who are incentivized have already worked out what their likely monetary reward is likely to be for the year and spend accordingly – they see it as part of their package and at worst this can only act as a demotivator if the monetary reward is reduced due to poor performance or a dip in the economy.

Spitzer's belief is that all individuals are driven by eight primary needs or human desires – all are important to us as human beings but some are more important than others.

We have based this short motivational diagnostic on Spitzer's Eight Human Desires. Complete the diagnostic following the instructions and you will be able to identify your top motivators. When these desires are satisfied, you will work at your best.

Motivation Self-assessment

Look at the list in Figure 5.5 and score each statement on a scale of 1 to 10 where 10 = extremely important to me and 1 = not very important to me at all.

Ensure that you spread your scores so ideally you should have no more than 4 questions with a 10, 4 questions with a 9, 4 questions with an 8, 4 questions with a 7, 4 with a score of 6, 4 with a score of 5, 4 with a score of 3, 4 questions with a score of 2, 4 questions with a score of 1.

		Your score out of 10
1	Having fun at work	
2	Feeling you have a stake in the organiszation's success	
3	Feeling in control of your own destiny	
4	Having opportunities to socialise	
5	Feeling competent at your job	
6	Succeeding at your work	
7	Receiving encouragement	
8	Being shown the significance of your work	
9	Being asked for your input	
10	Being able to make choices at work	
11	Being given responsibility for your work	
12	Working in a team with a powerful identity	
13	Using your hidden strengths	
14	Being allowed to set goals for yourself	
15	Being shown appreciation	
16	Knowing that what you do makes a difference	
17	Having variety at work	
18	Owning the work you do	
19	Being given leadership opportunities	
20	Being a valued member of a team	
21	Being given opportunities to learn and develop	

Figure 5.5   Motivation Self-assessment

22	Being encouraged to improve	
23	Being recognised for your effort	
24	Being able to relate your objectives to the bigger picture	
25	Feeling active and involved	
26	Feeling responsible for what you do	
27	Feeling empowered to make decisions	
28	Feeling you belong	
29	Being able to learn through mistakes	
30	Being challenged to stretch your limits	
31	Feeling rewarded for success	
32	Having meaning from your job	

Figure 5.5   *Concluded*

Transfer your scores to the grid below, shown in Figure 5.6. Then add the total of each category working across the page, e.g. for Category A total the sum of your scores for questions 1, 9, 17 and 25.

QUESTION NUMBER:	QUESTION NUMBER:	QUESTION NUMBER:	QUESTION NUMBER:	CATEGORY TOTAL
1	9	17	25	A
2	10	18	26	B
3	11	19	27	C
4	12	20	28	D
5	13	21	29	E
6	14	22	30	F
7	15	23	31	G
8	16	24	32	H

Figure 5.6   **Motivation Scoring**

Now write in the two categories in which you score the highest.

INTERPRETING YOUR SCORES

This questionnaire is designed to identify the work conditions which help you feel motivated. It works on the principle that motivation comes from within. Other people cannot motivate us. However, they can contribute to a motivating environment by satisfying one of the following needs that we may have:

Category A: activity: being active and involved at work, being kept busy with a variety of tasks

Category B: ownership: being able to own one's work and have responsibility

Category C: influence: being empowered, taking control, being able to influence

Category D: belonging: feeling part of a group and having opportunities to socialize

Category E: competency: feeling able to use and develop your skills further

Category F: achievement: feeling that goals are reached and there is a stretch in it for them

Category G: recognition: being recognized for effort and success

Category H: meaning: feeling that what you do has significance and is making a difference

Now that you have identified your top motivators, you may want to qualify that by thinking of situations where those desires have recently been met or have not been met and the impact of that on your levels of motivation.

This diagnostic can also be used with your team members. The very process of completing this as a team will appeal to those with a high need for affiliation and recognition so it can be a motivational tool in itself.

Here is a list of actions you may want to consider to satisfy each of the eight desires:

1.   Activity

   – Make work more active
   – Build fun into work
   – Ask for people's input
   – Add variety to work

2.   Ownership

   – Give people accountability and responsibility for tasks
   – Let people make choices more often

3.   Influence

   – Put people in positions of influence
   – Provide leadership opportunities

4.   Belonging

   – Offer opportunities to socialize
   – Create a powerful team identity

5.   Competence

   – Recognize people's strengths
   – Provide learning opportunities

6.   Achievement

   – Provide objective performance measures
   – Challenge people to stretch their limits

7.   Recognition

   – Provide encouragement
   – Show your appreciation

8.   Meaning

- Show people the significance and purpose of their work
- Help people see how they make a difference

Motivational Team Activity

It can be helpful to work through the following process:

- Ask the team to complete the questionnaire and reveal to others their top two or three scores.

- Remind everyone that all of the categories are motivators but the top two or three will be the most important to them.

- Explain to the team what each of the categories mean and ask them for examples of what they would need as team members for the needs of each category to be met.

- Ask each team member to identify what they would want more of or less of for them to feel their top desire was being met.

- Use this information as their leader to help you decide what you need to do in the future to appeal to each individual's desire.

De-motivators in the Workplace

It is also worth noting the aspects of the work environment which demotivate employees. This includes:

- Office politics

- Unclear expectations

- Unnecessary rules

- Poor processes

- Unproductive meetings

- Lack of follow-up

- Constant change

- Internal competition

- Dishonesty

- Hypocrisy

- Withholding information

- Discouraging responses

- Criticism

- Underutilization

- Tolerating poor performance

- Being taken for granted

- Over control

- Unfairness

- Imposed poor quality

- Inconsistency.

We suggest you discuss the items on this list with your team and identify the top two demotivators which you can then take steps to eliminate.

Motivation Self-evaluation Profile

In this chapter we have explored what is needed to create an empowering environment and tactics you can adopt as a leader to create that environment.

Dan Ariely is an Israeli American professor of psychology and behavioural economics at Duke University. In a talk he recently did at a TED conference he explains the results of some recent studies be completed around motivation. In one study he completed at Harvard University, he asked participants in two groups to build characters from LEGO®'s Bionicle series. In both groups, participants were paid decreasing amounts for each subsequent Bionicle, e.g. $3 for the first one, $2.70 for the second one etc. While one group's creations were stored under the table to be disassembled at the end of the experiment, the other group's Bionicles were disassembled as soon as they had built them.

The result was that the first group made 11 Bionicles, while the second group made 7 before they gave up. Even though there was no huge meaning at stake during this activity and even though the first group knew their work would be destroyed at the end of the experiment, seeing the results of their labour for even a short time was enough to dramatically improve the performance of the first group. Ariely had proof of the significance of achievement and recognition as a human desire.

This final questionnaire helps you identify strengths and gaps in your approach to creating an empowering environment.

Circle the number that you believe is closest to the way you currently behave to empower and create a motivating environment.

When you have finished, identify the questions where you have scored either one, two or three and create a plan of what you want to do to address these areas.

As an alternative, you can give the questionnaire in Figure 5.7 to your team to complete about you. When they have completed it, use it as a means of starting a discussion to understand from their perspective where you meet their expectations and where you need to improve.

	Never		Generally		Always
I help people to see the whole of which they are a part, to see how their work relates to the total situation, to broaden their perspective	1	2	3	4	5
I help to build purpose and meaning into the jobs of team members	1	2	3	4	5
I treat people with respect and dignity, irrespective of their performance on the job	1	2	3	4	5
I involve my team in creative participation in organiszational matters to (a) help them share in the contribution of ideas and (b) help them believe they are involved in worthwhile activity	1	2	3	4	5
I understand my own assumptions, viewpoints and attitudes and try to understand the assumptions, viewpoints and attitudes of my team members	1	2	3	4	5
I help my team to set realistic personal and work goals and try to provide the framework within which achievement of these goals becomes possible	1	2	3	4	5
I maintain a climate within which my team feel free to speak up and contribute ideas and suggestions. I give due credit to them for such ideas	1	2	3	4	5
I listen carefully to what my team and colleagues have to say before responding, and listen for what it tells me of their feelings as well as to the immediate meaning	1	2	3	4	5
I build and maintain a climate of mutual trust, confidence and respect in my area	1	2	3	4	5
I understand that people do not behave in uniform ways. I take into account the personal make-up and drivers of each person in my team and treat them accordingly	1	2	3	4	5
I recognise that many grievances arise because of poor communication so I make a special effort to maintain effective communication	1	2	3	4	5
I make a strong effort to set an example to my team	1	2	3	4	5
I ensure that job responsibilities and goals are clearly defined, understood, accepted and acted upon by my team	1	2	3	4	5
I try to best motivate my team to the highest achievement	1	2	3	4	5

Figure 5.7   Motivation Self-evaluation Profile

Chapter 6

Communication and Praise

In this chapter we outline the importance of constantly communicating about the customer to employees, both in terms of what is important to the customer as well as how individuals in the organization are performing in relation to customer expectations. We also spend time looking at the power of praise, which is often not recognized or practised by leaders, but which provides rich encouragement to employees to deliver above and beyond.

Communicate, Communicate, Communicate

One question we often ask leaders in organizations that want to become more customer-focused is how do you show that this matters? What leaders choose to communicate about the customer to their teams and how they do this makes a massive impact on team members' customer orientation.

If you stay behind your desk, are not approachable and do not make the effort to speak to team members or customers, do not expect to generate a culture of customer excellence. We saw a huge turnaround in attitude and approach to the customer when the Chief Financial Officer (CFO) of one of our client organizations started each of his business review meetings with the first agenda item: Customer. He asked each team to report back on what they were doing to provide and improve their service *before* he asked about financial results. The word quickly got round the business that the CFO was asking about customer service and that each departmental and business head needed to be prepared to stand up and be counted on this issue. The fact that the CFO continued this behaviour at the beginning of each meeting one year on really showed that it mattered. The culture of the organization began to change from this point and customer advocacy scores increased.

What do you say about your customers when you communicate to your team? How often does customer engagement form a key part of your communication? How much time do you personally spend with customers?

ACCESSIBLE, APPROACHABLE, CONNECTED

Leaders of today need to be more accessible, approachable and connected than ever before. There is a trend to increase the quantity of communication leaders have with their teams and the variety of communication methods. Outside organizations the 24/7 society and people's increasing use of digital means that people now expect to be informed and connected whenever they like. Communication within most organizations does not facilitate the responsiveness required by the demands of the digitally savvy employee. However, many organizations have become social in themselves and use internal social networks and communication and collaboration tools like 'Yammer' and 'Chatter' to speed up internal communications and reduce the amount of time taken up by email and meetings.

At insurance company LV= leaders continually communicate and make themselves accessible via a number of mediums, such as an internal communication and collaborative tool, coffee mornings to meet the Chief Executive, summer and Christmas social events, twice yearly Exec roadshows, managers' blogs and webcasts. They hold annual engagement surveys and act on employee ideas: 'You said, we did' and they also run a 'My Recognition' scheme which gathers 200 ideas a month (with the average reward per idea standing at £375).

LV= has learned that it needs to communicate regularly with all of its employees to ensure high levels of engagement and it needs to do this via a variety of methods. It weaves into its communication stories and examples of great customer service, such as when there was a flood at the port of Dover and employees found out which cars in the car park belonged to customers who were insured with them. They met customers off the ferries and explained that their cars were underwater but reassured them that LV= had already laid on repairs and had a suite of free hire cars waiting for them.

STORYTELLING

Storytelling is a powerful means of inspiring employees. It is the job of the leader to ensure that the communication is appealing and engaging for others. To help with this here are four questions leaders may find it useful to consider:

1.   What is the purpose of this communication – what is the key message I want to get across?

2.   What do I want my people/audience to think, do and feel at the end of the message?

3.   How am I going to make it personal?

4.   How do I want to be remembered?

This allows you to consider the three key influences when you are communicating – the message, the recipient of that message and yourself, the deliverer of that message.

The purpose of making the story personal is that it gives the leader an opportunity to express how they are feeling and thinking about the message – it allows the audience to see the person behind the message and engage with them. It allows the leader to reveal something about them that is a demonstration of their humanity so that others are attracted to that person. Placing you in the story is an essential part of making your communication engaging and memorable. This is not about earning a reputation as a great orator, it is about earning a reputation as an authentic, human communicator.

> *One story I heard from a manager at the supermarket chain Sainsbury's was about a three-and-a-half-year-old girl who with the help of her parents wrote to the retailer. She was confused by one of Sainsbury's products called tiger bread. In her eyes, the bread didn't resemble a tiger at all and in fact looked very much like a giraffe. To her surprise, the customer support manager (age 27-and-one-third) told her that he couldn't agree more. Knowing the customer was certainly right in this instance – and spotting an unusual opportunity to do something fun – Sainsbury's changed the name of the bread and put signs around their stores that give a humorous nod to the three-and-a-half-year-old's original idea. The story went viral and the retailer saw a huge increase in sales of giraffe bread.*

To what extent do you talk about customers and great service in the communication you have with your team and other employees? Do you communicate stories about service heroes and recognize team members who go above and beyond for the customer? Do you share good practice and news of improvements and innovations that employees have undertaken to better serve the customer?

COMMUNICATIONS CHECKLIST

Use the checklist in Figure 6.1 to assess what you can start to do or do more of.

	In place	Start or do more of
I put customer service at the start of every meeting agenda		
I regularly spend time with customers		
I hold regular team meetings where I talk about the customer		
When I visit another team or department I make a point of talking to team members		
I engage my team members in conversation about their experience of dealing with customers		
I have personally served a customer in the past three months		
I have shared a story about how someone has delivered great service in the past three months		
I use a variety of medium to communicate to employees about the customer		
I have written a blog about customer service in the past three months		
I regularly provide feedback the results of customer surveys to my team		
I seek feedback from my team on my communication style		

Figure 6.1   Communication Checklist

COMMUNICATION STYLE

If you have not done so already, we recommend that you also ask for some feedback on your communication style and its impact. There are two sets of influence behaviours that individuals generally adopt at work to communicate effectively: Push and Pull behaviours. Push behaviours include:

- proposing – giving views and opinions, making proposals

- directing – stating what you need and expect of others

- evaluating – ideas and opinions given to you by others

- incentivizing – providing incentives to do something or giving the consequences of not doing something.

People who use predominantly push behaviours work from their own agenda. At the extreme they may be viewed by others as 'pushy' or aggressive. Their language is very much centred on 'I' – 'I want', 'I need'. The impact of their behaviour is that they signal that they want the person they are interacting with to move their opinion or to change.

The consequence of too much 'push' can be that people on the receiving end become disenfranchised. They do not consider that their opinions are sought or valued. In extreme a push style can appear dictatorial. The result of this style of behaviour is that team members lose respect and trust for their leader.

Pull behaviours, on the other hand, focus more on the other person:

- Enquiring – asking questions to find out more from the person

- Listening and pacing – actively listening, summarizing. Matching the pace of the other person, going with their flow

- Finding areas of agreement – building common ground, 'yes and' rather than 'yes but'

- Being open about your limitations and being open to suggestions and ideas – being ready to admit mistakes, being open to other ways of doing things.

These behaviours focus on the other person: the leader listens to the speaker. The speaker will be using pull language like 'you' and 'we'. People using pull behaviours show an interest in and consideration for the individual. The impact of using a pull style of influence is to signal that you are prepared to change. You are working from the other person's agenda. However, if you adopt a predominantly pull style of influence all the time you may be perceived as 'a push over' or passive person.

In order to communicate effectively with customers and team members, therefore, customer leaders need to adopt a style where both push and pull are given equal balance. It is particularly useful in conflict situations and situations where you wish to gain buy-in to use pull behaviours before push, e.g. use enquiry, listening and pacing techniques with the other person. Equally in these situations it is important to be direct about one's own views and opinions:

> 'What do you think about the feedback we've received from customers this month?' (pull question)

> 'So from what you're saying you believe ...' (listening and pacing – pull technique)

> 'I agree that there has to be a better way of doing this ...' (pull – finding areas of agreement)

> 'The one area I need you to focus on is ...' (push – directing).

A mixture of push and pull styles of communication helps move the conversation forward and gains agreement.

Feedback and Recognition

Great service organizations consistently and constantly provide customer feedback to their team members. They make the team aware of what customers like about the service they receive and where they'd like to see improvements. They recognize individuals who go above and beyond to deliver exceptional service.

When was the last time you said: 'well done', 'great job', or even 'fabulous' or 'excellent' to someone? Businesses with a strong customer focus recognize team members who deliver exceptional service from across the business – no matter whether they are front-line facing or sit in a support function.

According to a 2009 report from McKinsey, a $1,000 payment had ten times more return on investment when given through a recognition programme than when added to base pay. Another study by White Water Consulting Inc., found an impact of a 1 per cent pay increase can be achieved through frequent thanks and praise.

The Power of Praise

The US Department of Labor found that the number one reason people leave their jobs is because they 'do not feel appreciated'. And the majority of us don't give or receive anywhere near the amount of praise that we should. As a result, we're much less productive, and in many cases, completely disengaged in our jobs.

The concepts of 'recognition' and 'praise' are two critical components for creating positive emotions in organizations. Gallup research of more than 10,000 business units and more than 30 industries has found that individuals who receive regular recognition and praise:

- increase their individual productivity

- increase engagement among their colleagues

- are more likely to stay with their organization

- receive higher loyalty and satisfaction scores from customers

- have better safety records and fewer accidents on the job.

People want recognition; they want to be noticed and appreciated. A manager who praises is one who's paying attention to the work as well as the worker. This personalized attention creates an emotional bond between employees and the organization. This goes a long way in developing engagement and encouraging people to give of their best. It also puts money in the employee emotional piggy bank which they can take out when times are difficult or tough, provided of course that the praise is frequently applied (at least once a week).

On the flip side, one study of healthcare workers found that when employees were working for a boss they disliked and who did not give them any praise, they had significantly higher blood pressure.

There is something memorable about being recognized at just the right time, by just the right person, with just the right words. The thing about praise is that it needs to be heartfelt. The words themselves can be short but the tone and sincerity with which they are said make all the difference:

- Well done

- Thank you

- We could not have done it without you

- I trust you

- I'm proud of you

- I'm glad to have you as part of our team

- Great idea! Let's go with it.

- You have made a significant contribution to ___.

- You really helped me out

- You are a star!

- This is one of the best I've seen

- We couldn't have done it without you

- You have set a new standard of excellence for us all to strive toward

- I really appreciate what you have done.

Fewer than one in three workers, according to Gallup research, can strongly agree that they've received *any* praise from a team leader, manager or supervisor in the last seven days. The same research showed that employees who report that they're not adequately recognized at work are three times more likely to say they'll quit in the next year.

WHY DO WE YEARN PRAISE?

People need a day-to-day feeling of being appreciated and recognized for what they do. The desire for appreciation and having interest shown in you stems from a chemical reaction in our bodies. This chemical is dopamine, a neurotransmitter produced in the brain. Recognition for good work releases dopamine in the brain, which creates feelings of pride and pleasure. Dopamine stimulates the ventral striatum and nucleus accumbens, the parts of the brain that process rewards and create positive emotions like satisfaction and enjoyment. Evolutionary biologists think dopamine helped drive humans' ability to learn and survive, so the desire for dopamine is biologically preordained and humans' attempt to get it is inevitable.

Furthermore, knowledge that by repeating the behaviour you will receive more praise results in further dopamine being released, thus reinforcing the behaviour. The dopamine kick people get from praise doesn't last very long, so it takes repeated exposure to build the a pattern of behaviour. This is why holding an annual performance appraisal does not often provide the recognition people seek. Praising at least once a week is far more effective.

WHY IS IT SO DIFFICULT TO GIVE PRAISE?

When we consider the positive impact of praise on the employee's emotional piggy bank, we are surprised that more managers do not use praise and recognition to encourage a culture of exceptional service. However, research studies also point to the negativity bias. The brain is set up to notice the negative first. Several studies, for example, have found that people noticed pictures of 'frowny' faces more often than 'smiley' faces. As service leaders our tendency therefore is to pick up what some has *not* been doing or achieved, rather than successful behaviours and work.

Some managers worry that they can give employees too much recognition, but the research shows that it's extremely difficult to do that, as long as the recognition is right for the person. Other managers say that they don't receive recognition themselves so why should they give praise to others when they are only doing the job that was expected of them. This rather defeatist approach flies in the face of all the research studies which show the power of recognition. In our view providing praise and motivational feedback is a key reinforcement of positive customer-orientated behaviours. It builds confidence and pride. Other managers are concerned about showing favouritism to a minority of people. We do not see this as favouritism, rather as identifying positive role models who will be respected by their colleagues for the behaviours they demonstrate.

If you have a personal barrier to giving praise, a useful tip to overcome this is to make yourself give one piece of praise to a different person each day. Look for the positives. One leader we know put five mints in their pocket at the beginning of each week – these were his favourite sweets. He set himself the challenge of giving a piece of recognition each day and could only eat a mint when he had done so.

SO WHAT IS THE BEST FORM OF PRAISE?

There is no 'best' form of praise. Different employees have different preferences. All of them need frequent praise and some need it more publicly than others, in front of the group or the whole company. A further consideration is whether to give individual praise or praise a whole team. It's a huge thing to feel connected and one of the ways of doing that is to get recognition as a group. Publicly recognizing whole departments for the value they add to the organization increases employee engagement, raises awareness of the department's achievements in the organization and provides the buzz employees get from recognition.

EXAMPLE RECOGNITION SCHEME

One organization we work with has a scheme that encourages, motivates and rewards staff for 'living' the key behaviours that underpin their desired culture. Customers and colleagues nominate staff when they have received excellent customer service. Encouraging employees to nominate their colleagues reaffirms that delivering excellent customer service internally is just as important as external customer service – what happens internally has a knock-on effect for customers.

All the nominations are reviewed at the end of the month by a committee of managers and a winner for each region is selected.

For some people what is important is recognition from their peers they most respect, while some desire nothing more than a quiet word of praise in private. So how can you determine the right sort of praise for each employee? The best way to find out is to ask.

Recognition schemes can be controversial and it is important to ensure that they are seen to be fair. We favour those where peer as well as line manager and customer nominations can be made. We work with one organization who brings customers in to be the final judges of the nominations for service excellence.

KEY QUESTIONS AROUND RECOGNITION

Some questions to consider when designing a recognition scheme are:

1. WHO should be rewarded and recognized? – The company as a whole, groups or individuals?

2. WHY should they be recognized? – e.g. for outstanding performance or improvement in customer experience?

3. WHEN should this happen? On a one-off or ongoing basis, e.g. as part of a regular reward scheme or performance management system?

4. WHAT form should the recognition take? e.g. financial or non-financial reward?

5. HOW should the scheme be administered? e.g. what should be the method of delivering the reward/recognition?

Top Tips on Recognition Actions

I. SURVEY YOUR TEAM

It is surprising how many organizations assume they know best when it comes to recognizing staff. Well-conducted surveys are a critical means to challenge assumptions.

First Direct believes it must continue to work at understanding its employees and the culture more deeply. It has introduced a Culture Critique, using staff focus groups and one-to-one interviews not just with current employees but past ones too.

2. TAILOR SERVICE AWARDS TO INDIVIDUAL NEEDS

Recognition through token or monetary benefits has got to be meaningful to those who receive it. American Express, for example found that the majority of employees considered time off work the most significant form of reward. They implemented a recognition scheme called 'Time Off Vouchers' where individuals can be given time off in recognition for achievement.

3. INSTIGATE A 'JOB WELL DONE AWARD'

Sometimes immediate recognition for everyday good service can do a power of good. One car retailer runs a 'WOW' scheme where anyone within the organization can send a 'WOW' card to a member of staff who has gone out of their way to give them good service. At the end of each month, the number of 'WOW' cards are counted. Those people with the most number of cards win M&S vouchers as a thank you.

4. REGULARLY FEEDBACK CUSTOMER COMMENTS AND COMPLIMENTS

Tyre company Kwik-Fit keeps a customer correspondence folder in each depot reception area, publicizing positive letters customers have written. It rings up customers on a daily basis to gain feedback and publicizes the results internally.

5. ISSUE CERTIFICATES OF ACHIEVEMENT

When employees attain defined customer experience standards and skill levels, a certificate or token award can help to demonstrate its importance. A certificate of achievement can become highly prized.

6. PUBLICIZE EXAMPLES OF GOOD SERVICE

Every service job has a substantial routine element, and a company newsletter or email should give service contribution the recognition it deserves; sometimes good sales figures seem to be the only thing to get recognized and people could be forgiven for thinking that service mistakes are the only thing to get noticed. To promote good practice, regular newsletter features on success stories can be a big help to the individuals concerned and to others.

Unipart ran an award scheme called 'Mark in Action Award' which recognized individuals and teams who took exceptional actions to look after internal and external customers. Any customer or Unipart employee could nominate another Unipart employee for the award if service was beyond the call of duty. To date over half the nominations have been for internal service. There is a rigorous verification process by a panel of judges. Selected award winners are invited to monthly formal ceremonies attended by board directors and senior managers. They receive a token number of shares in the company, gold lapel pins and have photos in reception area. Winners have also been featured in annual reports and accounts.

7. GIVE EACH TEAM AN ALLOWANCE

Giving a sum of discretionary money, say £1000 a year to teams to distribute in agreed ways can help promote a healthy, empowered environment. The team should be able to choose to distribute lots of small awards or fewer larger ones. One company we worked with promised each team member £150 each of activities if the whole company achieved its NPS target. The only proviso was that the money should be spent as a team on whatever activity the group decided. Other ideas include non-monetary discretionary awards, such as retail vouchers and team t-shirts to record achievements. One manager of an IT service centre says 'a little thing like taking the trouble to buy ice-creams for everyone on a hot busy day lifts spirits; it's the thought that counts'.

8. INSTIGATE AN AWARD FOR GOOD SERVICE TO THE INTERNAL CUSTOMER

Many organizations put all their focus on the external customer and neglect the needs of the internal customer. Yet a lot of the frustrations of front-line service staff can be traced back to the departments who support them. These departments are often far removed from the external customer and may well put up defensive barriers which hinder free-flowing processes. At Birmingham Midshires Building Society the employee annual bonus, for example, was linked to the attainment of an agreed level of customer satisfaction. This was determined by the building society's customer survey.

9. INCLUDE CUSTOMER EXPERIENCE IN PERFORMANCE MANAGEMENT

Performance management should explicitly hold employees accountable for service delivery. In organizations such as Boots the Chemist, customer experience is a key measurement in performance appraisal. Sales assistants are assessed on two critical competences, being proactive and building positive relations with customers. Other organizations specifically link performance bonus to the attainment of customer satisfaction targets.

10. DEVELOP CUSTOMER EXPERIENCE COMPETENCIES AND ENSURE CAREER PROGRESSION IS LINKED TO GOOD SERVICE

Defining service competencies is the first step in setting out well-defined improvement and development targets. National Vocational Qualifications in Customer Experience are becoming more widespread and increasingly accepted as a valuable transferable qualification.

Is Your Employee Recognition Effective?

You have a key role to play as a leader in recognizing excellent service behaviours. Use this checklist to identify improvements in the way you praise and recognize. Answer Yes or No to the following questions:

- In the past seven days have you given someone at work some recognition or praise?

- Was the last praise you gave personalized according to the person's interests and motivations?

- Was it timely and genuine?

- Do you give praise at least once a week?

- Do you make time at team or management meetings for people to talk about successes and things that are going well?

- Do you use a hand-written thank you note or thoughtful email to give praise as well as face-to-face thanks and recognition?

- Do you share praise for an employee with their co-workers where appropriate?

- Do you use a range of non-monetary forms of recognition such as job flexibility, opportunities for training and development and time off?

- Do you provide the same or similar recognition for similar achievement for all employees?

- Is the recognition and reward you use appropriate in size to the level of effort and achievement?

- Do you encourage peers to recognize one another?

- Do you provide specific examples of employees' accomplishments so that it's clear how they are role models for others?

- Do you recognize employees for developing new ideas or showing initiative?

- Do you engage senior leaders in delivering awards and recognition as well as yourself?

Now consider where you have answered 'no' and select one area where you can make an improvement in how you recognize. We hope that this chapter has demonstrated the importance of praise and that you are motivated to put what you have learned in to action to create a climate of great customer service.

Chapter 7
Improve and Innovate

In this chapter we look at the important topics of service improvements and service innovation. We'll look at how complaints are an important source of improvement ideas and how you can engage your team in identifying and driving up service standards. We'll also look at some of the trends that may impact you and your organization around the customer experience of the future and which will encourage innovation.

Use Customer Feedback to Drive Improvements

Customer's expectations are constantly rising. To continue to be successful businesses today need to innovate and improve constantly. This means being aware of trends and finding novel ways to deliver an exceptional customer experience.

CUSTOMER INSIGHTS

Customer insights are a rich source of improvement ideas. Irrespective of the means by which you gather insights – for example via customer satisfaction surveys, Twitter feeds, feedback from focus groups or one-to-one discussions with customers – customer feedback can provide your business with a clear picture of what you are doing well and where you need to improve. It's really important to establish in whatever feedback you gather, what is important to customers as well as how satisfied they are and what you can do to improve. As Figure 7.1 illustrates, areas of high importance to customers but low satisfaction to customers offer businesses hidden opportunities.

```
HIGH
            ┌──────────────────┬──────────────────┐
 S          │                  │                  │
 A          │                  │                  │
 T          │    EXPENDABLE    │     MAINTAIN     │
 I          │                  │                  │
 S          │                  │                  │
 F          │                  │                  │
 A          ├──────────────────┼──────────────────┤
 C          │                  │                  │
 T          │                  │       MINE       │
 I          │    REDUNDANT     │      HIDDEN      │
 O          │                  │   OPPORTUNITIES  │
 N          │                  │                  │
            └──────────────────┴──────────────────┘
LOW      LOW                                    HIGH
                     IMPORTANCE
```

Figure 7.1   Importance Versus Satisfaction

Customer Journey Mapping and Process Improvement

Another method of creating a customer focus is looking at the processes your organization adopts from a customer's perspective. How easy is your company to do business with? Mapping the steps in a process can help identify blockages to excellent customer experience such as time delays or lengthy approval procedures. An extension of this technique is customer journey mapping, which we discussed in more detail in Chapter 3.

Complaints as a Driver of Business Improvement

> *Your most unhappy customers are your greatest source of learning.*
>
> *Bill Gates*

Do not forget that complaints can drive business improvement, improve internal communications and increase operational efficiency. In Australia, a study by the Public Transportation Ombudsman into the taxi and hire car industry in the state of Victoria found that when complaints were viewed positively and handled professionally and non-defensively, they drove industry improvement. This in turn led to fewer dissatisfied customers, increased customer loyalty and greater confidence in the industry.

The amount of customer complaints is on the rise and is a clear indicator of a growing refusal to put up with poor service; yet many companies have failed to act on the consequences and are losing customers and reputations as a result. Research in the UK by the Institute of Customer Service reveals this rising customer trend: around three-quarters of customers are prepared to complain, compared with about half around 10 years ago.

Complaints handled well enhance a brand's reputation. A complaining customer who experiences a good recovery from their problem will become a promoter of the organization and build positive word of mouth (and clicks), openly spreading positive stories about their experience. Studies show that a 5 per cent reduction in the customer defection rate can increase profits by 25 to 85 per cent, depending on the industry (US Technical Assistance Research Program [TARP] Studies 2010).

A survey by American Express in the UK showed that more than half of customers would spend more on goods and services if the service experience was guaranteed to be first class. Handling complaints well is one way of ensuring exceptional customer loyalty.

Depending on the industry, 54 to 70 per cent of customers who register a complaint will do business again with the organization if their complaint is resolved in a timely and thoughtful fashion. This figure rises to 95 per cent if the customer feels that the complaint was resolved quickly and fairly: in fact a well-handled complaint tends to breed more customer loyalty than they had before the negative incident.

SOME TELLING STATISTICS

- Of the three out of four customers who are dissatisfied and do not complain directly to the organization, at least half just stop buying or dealing with the organization where they have a choice.

- On average a dissatisfied customer tells at least 10 other people about their poor experience, whereas they only tell 3 people if they have a good experience as a customer. The 10 people who have heard about the poor experience from the customer tell at least 5 other people.

- Only the minority of customers who are dissatisfied do in fact complain at the time of the incident. This is often likened to an iceberg: underneath the waterline are the vast majority of customers who do not complain.

- The Internet and social media are fundamentally changing the landscape. Jeff Bezos of Amazon.com says if you make customers unhappy in the physical world, they might each tell six friends. If you make customers unhappy on the Internet, they can each tell 6,000 friends.

THE PERILS OF HANDLING COMPLAINTS BADLY

In a disturbingly large number of cases in organizations this message does not get translated into action. Only about 50 per cent of complainants report a satisfactory resolution to their problem. The reasons are complex. Many organizations have a culture which contains elements of unclear priorities, complacency, blame or cover-up, and this leads to problems being buried or ignored. This can display itself in front-line staff, for example, failing to tell management of customer issues for fear that they personally will get the blame. At its worst, it can lead to customer dissatisfaction building and management blissfully unaware of the problem until perhaps a news story breaks of an unhappy customer.

Sometimes cumbersome procedures lead customers to simply give up making an official complaint. Another factor is the difficulty of fostering and maintaining a customer-focused culture and processes where mistakes are encouraged to be reported and acted upon.

Some companies have failed to take on board that customers have become more empowered and are no longer prepared to accept poor service. People have become more travelled and better informed, with an increasing demand for international brands and corresponding service experience. Perhaps the most notable influence is the rapid growth of social media. Increasingly people throughout the globe are using tablets and phones to access the Internet. It is estimated that between 500 million and 1 billion people will access financial services by mobile phone (tap and go) in the next five years to make payments and transfers.

New communication channels are altering customers' expectations about service. Social media is giving customers a vehicle for spreading good and bad news at the click of a mouse. Aggregator sites such as TripAdvisor, Amazon and Feefo which constantly provide customer feedback are examples of how customers can shape future purchasing choices. Research from Euro RSCG Worldwide shows that nearly 43 per cent of US Internet users feel less inhibited online, with the effect most prominent among females and users aged 25 to 54. In the research customers reported they were also more likely to 'lash out' on the Web when they had something to say about a company or brand.

Give attention to identifying the root cause of a complaint, anticipating and resolving a number of key problem areas. It is clear that a company's reputation and business growth can be substantially promoted by effective complaint handling.

Involve Your Team

Importantly, engage your team in improvement ideas and actions. People who are closest to the customer have a great deal of knowledge about what works or not for the customer, and they can usually tell you how things can be improved.

Insurance company Aviva has established the Aviva Customer Cup competition. Here 550 teams from across the business compete to identify and implement service improvements. There are three rounds of judging and then the top ten teams present their ideas to the Board. (One winning team reviewed the pay-out on the maturity bonds process and improved this from 29–65 days to 2–5 days, honing 12 customer touch points down to 2. As a result there was an improvement in Net Promoter Score of 39 points to +61 out of 100.)

Symantec is one of the world's largest software companies with more than 18,500 employees in more than 50 countries and one of its products, Norton Security, has 120 million customers worldwide. Norton had a goal of cutting the need for customers to contact the company directly with queries by 25 per cent and to cut call wait-time to a maximum of 2 minutes. It achieved these objectives over two years. It improved customer satisfaction scores to 90 per cent and Net Promoter Scores by +10 points by involving its team members in ideas for improvement to its customers' Web experience. This involved:

- Making navigation easier.

- Setting up a smarter virtual agent called Nathan: he copes with 300,000 questions from customers. If Nathan can't help, he directs the customer to the self-help page.

- Increasing the use of social media – actively responding to 'tweets'.

It also made improvements to the support it provides customers online by:

- Providing a faster service by telling customers when peak times were

- Providing better agent tools

- Holding customer focus groups to find out their needs

- Using an online feedback survey to measure NPS

- Simplifying the way live support is used.

Create a Service Improvement Plan

One of the techniques we've seen work well in driving improvements is the creation of a service improvement plan. This sets out the key priority improvements (no more than three or four at one time) that the team agrees to address. Importantly the plan is more likely to be implemented if the team knows this will be formally reviewed and recognition given for success.

Innovation

The challenge for all businesses is to not only improve their customer experience but also to transform the way that they deliver service to the customer. In order to innovate businesses need to understand the environment in which they operate as well as consumer trends.

Mapping Your Landscape

A useful starting point as a leader is to take time out with your peers or team to map the landscape in which you operate. Organizations are impacted by two sets of external factors: the macro and micro environment. Sometimes called the near and the far environment, these forces for change can be summarized as in Figure 7.2.

Figure 7.2   The Macro and Micro Environment

PESTEL

The far or macro environment relates to factors which are:

- Political

- Economic

- Sociocultural

- Technological

- Environmental

- Legal

These influences may impact your business, now or in the future. Political influences relate to government or constitutional policies that may affect your business. Economic influences relate to the economy as a whole. Sociocultural influences encompass such factors as class, age and gender as well as issues such as culture and diversity. Technological influences include the use of the Internet, social media etc. Many businesses are impacted today by environmental issues. Legal constraints also affect business performance.

PESTEL EXERCISE

List the potential influences that may impact your business in the next 1–2 years (Figure 7.3).

• Political	
• Economic	
• Socio-cultural	
• Technological	

Figure 7.3   PESTEL Exercise

• Environmental	
• Legal	

Figure 7.3   *Concluded*

Next consider the implications of these factors on your business.

The Near Environment

An audit of the near external environment involves analyzing customers and the competitive marketplace as well as being aware of suppliers and other stakeholders' requirements. There are a number of tools you can use to do this. One of the most widely used is called *Porter's Five Forces*.

Michael Porter, a business professor from Harvard, first developed the Five Forces of Industry model in the late 1970s. Each of the model's five components have measurable components which classify each force as having a 'Low', 'Moderate', or 'High' strength.

1.   Bargaining power of suppliers,

2.   Bargaining power of buyers (customers),

3.   Threat of new entrants,

4.   Threat of substitutes, and

5.   Intensity of competitive rivalry.

The collective strength of the five forces then determines how attractive the industry is to potential entrants. According to Vordbera in the book *Strategic Management*, the ideal industry to operate in would have a 'low' strength for all five forces.

Use Porter's Five Forces To Analyse Your Marketplace

Strength?	High?	Medium?	Low?
(1) Bargaining Power of Suppliers			
(2). Bargaining Power of Buyers (customers)			
(3) Threat of New Entrants			
(4) Threat of Substitutes			
(5) Intensity of Competitive Rivalry			

Figure 7.4   Analyse Your Marketplace

• Given your analysis, what conclusions can you draw about your marketplace and the threats this may present in the future?

• What mitigating action if any can you take to minimize the high or medium strengths?

Trends in Customer Experience

At the same time as recognizing the landscape in which you are currently operating, it is important to also stay abreast of trends in customers' expectations. Being aware of these trends helps you anticipate customer needs and can drive innovation.

Omni-channel

A very clear trend for example which is affecting every business is the rising use by customers of omni-channels to interact with organizations. As we've seen today's consumer wants 24/7 access to products and services and they want to interact with businesses via whatever channel they choose. This trend has implications for the way businesses invest their resources in the future as well as how they ensure a consistency of service. Customers expect to be able to click and collect, come into branch, use webchat, Skype or the phone for example whenever is convenient to them. And they expect you to know their preferences and to be able to mix channels seamlessly and with the minimum of effort.

How is and will this growing trend impact you and your team? What can you do to better manage and meet this demand as well as staying ahead of the trend?

Location-specific Trends

In whatever country you are reading this book, you also need to be aware of the demographic trends that will impact your business. The following extracts come with permission from KPMG's website on a page headed: *How will demographic trends affect the retail sector?* which was posted in July 2013. It is reproduced by permission of the KPMG/Ipsos Retail Think Tank (RTT). RTT was founded by KPMG and Ipsos Retail Performance (formerly Synovate) in February 2006. It now meets quarterly to provide authoritative 'thought leadership' on matters affecting the retail industry.

We are conscious that these trends relate specifically to the UK but we hope even if your business does not operate in this country that it will serve to illustrate some of the types of trends you may need to be aware of and discover about customers in your country.

Demographic Trends: the Head and Tail of the Snake

If you see life as a snake, in the UK and Western Europe it would certainly have a large head and tail!

The UK population is growing and projected to rise to 73.2 million in 2035, creating new market demand and a growing marketplace. The ageing population and changing ethnic make-up of the UK are two of the most influential demographic forces shaping the UK consumer market.

Over the next ten years two-thirds of all retail spending growth will come from those aged 55 and over. The main challenge for customer experience professionals will be adapting to the ageing population. By 2030, the number aged 65 or older is projected to reach 15.5 million, growing by 43 per cent on its level in 2012, compared to an expansion of only 13 per cent in the population as a whole. While this group currently accounts for less than £1 in every £5 of total spending, this share might rise to £1 in every £4 within two decades.

An ageing population profile, helped by lower birth rates, longer life expectancy and the sheer size of the baby-boomer generation – many of whom are now retiring – are just three factors underpinning this trend. As a result, Office of National Statistics estimate that over the next ten years almost two-thirds of all retail spending growth will come from those aged over 55.

Older shoppers are far more demanding than the young both in terms of better service and accessibility. In addition online shopping is becoming more widespread amongst the older population. Analysts predict shopping facilities that assist mobility and convenience will continue to grow, as will delivery services. Health, DIY and home maintenance, which attract a large share of elderly households' budgets, should benefit from this change. Clothing, beer and soft drinks, which are geared towards a more youthful market, could lose out. Product design, service delivery, marketing and advertising will all have to be rethought to become more appealing to an older demographic. Above all, there will be the challenge of appealing to older consumers who still think of themselves as young consumers.

Older Consumers are Down-ageing

The baby boomer generation has no intention of retiring quietly to a life of crochet and gentle gardening. They are down-ageing: acting younger, both physically and mentally. Understanding this is important because it is this older segment that's going to drive expectations of service over the next 10 years.

Silver Sloggers

However, contrary to conventional wisdom, baby-boomers are not all awash with disposable income. With ultra-low interest rates and annuity rates, pension income is under considerable pressure, forcing many older consumers back onto the part-time job market to supplement their financial resources. One painful consequence of people living longer is that many older consumers have the cost of looking after their own parents to consider, and their own children may not find it easy to get full-time jobs in a continuing climate of financial austerity.

The number of people aged 65 and over who are working has doubled in the past two decades, coining the term 'Silver Sloggers'. Older consumers will unquestionably be different from today with marked differences in lifestyle, attitude and preferences.

The Rise of Generation Y

The rising influence of so-called 'Generation Y', who are generally considered to be the under 35 and born roughly between 1980 and 2000 will also have a major impact on customer experience.

Not only does this group desire different products from previous generations, but it has different ways of shopping and different attitudes to brands. The changes already underway in multichannel retailing will particularly appeal to this generation.

Consumers in this age group are ubiquitous users of digital technology across multiple mobile platforms. Research by Accenture shows that Generation Y consumers own on average between three and four digital devices per person, and 27 per cent own more than four devices. They also spend an average of six to six-and-a-half hours per day using a digital device for personal activities including messaging/texting (48 per cent), emailing (39 per cent), getting news (27 per cent) and shopping for a product or service online (20 per cent).

Generation Z

The number of children aged 16 and under in the UK is projected to increase by 12 per cent to 13 million by 2035. This means a difficult balancing act for customer experience professionals. While tackling the demands of the baby-boomers, they must look at the other end of the age spectrum and work out how to attract the interest, and spending power, of the younger generation.

Too young to remember 9/11, these under-16s have grown up in a world in political and financial turmoil. As a result, they are keen to look after their money, and make the world a better place. This generation is described as the 'first tribe of true digital natives' or 'screenagers'. But unlike the older

Generation Y, they are smarter, safer, more mature and want to change the world. Their pin-up is Malala Yousafzai, the Pakastani education campaigner who survived being shot by the Taliban.

They are worthy, keen to volunteer and aware that an education is to be treasured. Research by US advertising agency Sparks & Honey says 60 per cent of them want to have an impact on the world, compared with 39 per cent of Generation Y.

Shift in Britain's Multicultural Make-up

A further trend is the rise in ethnic communities, particularly in urban areas. Net migration has become the primary driver of demographic change in the UK. However, change is not being felt uniformly and differs by region. Figures from the Office for National Statistics show that in the year in the year to 30 June 2012 a third of migrants entering the UK headed to London, demonstrating the city's rapidly changing ethnic profile. Half the babies born in London are now to non-indigenous UK mothers. Customer experience professionals will need to identify the kind of service a less 'English' population will need in the next decade.

Smaller Households

Similarly, there is predicted to be more but smaller households. The number of one-person households in England is forecast to increase, single-parent households are forecast to continue to rise, while the number of one-child households is growing and now accounts for 47 per cent, increasing demand for smaller pack sizes and increasing the spend per child.

Urban Density

In 1950, the population living in UK cities was 79 per cent – already a large figure – but one which is set to rise to 92.2 per cent by 2030. The UK's overall population density is one of the highest in the world at 256 people per square kilometre, due to the particularly high population density in England. Almost one-third of the population currently lives in England's south-east which is predominantly urban and suburban, with about 8 million in London.

This concentration in urban centres means that half the population of UK now shop for comparison goods in just 90 or so major trading locations nationally, down from over 200 in 1971. This steady market concentration has gone hand-in-hand with the homogenization of offers in large dominant centres simply because mass market non-food retailers are all chasing space in the same urban places.

Local Community

At the same time consumers are looking for local connections and accessibility. Grocers are following a completely different strategy, consolidating network penetration by opening large numbers of small convenience goods branches, increasing rather than reducing branch network sizes. Analysts predict the growth of local services such as GP surgeries, libraries and other health services which have already begun to pop up in between convenience stores and chemists whereas traditionally they have been set back from the main thoroughfare. These act as a draw for the older generation who are less inclined and perhaps less able to travel for their groceries but still need to access essential local services. Transport, accessibility and local infrastructure will therefore become increasingly important to the older generation.

The financial and time demands being placed on the middle generation is growing, due to an increasing number of dependent children staying at home for longer and a rise in the elderly being cared for at home. This is placing a further squeeze on disposable income and a growing demand for convenience-led local solutions. Analysts predict that as urbanization increases, consumers will increasingly look to connect to local communities.

Concern for Privacy and Lack of Trust

Consumers are demanding a more individual and personalized service. Asked to rank the factors that would make them most likely to complete the purchase of a product or service in a 2014 survey by Accenture, respondents' top three choices were sales and competitive pricing (61 per cent), superior products (36 per cent) and personalized customer experience – both online and in store (35 per cent).

Customer loyalty programmes and relevant promotions followed, at 31 and 26 per cent, respectively, but engaging advertising campaigns and celebrity endorsements trailed far behind, at 6 per cent and 3 per cent, respectively.

The vast majority (80 per cent) of consumers aged 20–40 in the US and the UK believe total privacy in the digital world is a thing of the past, and in the same Accenture study nearly half (49 per cent) said they would not object to having their buying behaviour tracked if it would result in relevant offers from brands and suppliers.

However, according to the survey, the majority of consumers are concerned about the use of their personal information: 87 per cent believe adequate safeguards are not in place to protect their personal information and 64 per cent are concerned about websites tracking their buying behaviour.

More than half (56 per cent) say they are trying to safeguard their privacy by inputting their credit card information each time they make an online purchase rather than having that data stored for future use.

Seventy percent of respondents believe businesses aren't transparent about how their information is being used, and 68 per cent say there is not enough transparency around what is being done with their information.

This lack of trust is driving consumers further to rely upon peer-to-peer recommendation rather than brand marketing:

- A recent survey for Consumer Focus found that more than 62 per cent of consumers trust what other consumers tell them more than what companies say

- Research by BT and Avaya found that 51 per cent trust the advice on review sites more than an organization's official website

- Research from the USA by Nielsen found that 68 per cent of social media users go to social networking sites to read consumer feedback on products and services, with over half using these sites to provide product feedback, both positive and negative. Nielsen research also found that consumers trusted consumer online reviews and personal recommendations from friends and acquaintances far more than brand advertising.

- A 2012 survey of Internet users in Britain by Reevoo found that 88 per cent of consumers consult reviews when making a purchase, and 60 per cent said they were more likely to purchase from a site that has customer reviews.

So the customer is far more in charge of the buying process than ever before. This phenomenon is just as prevalent in the business-to-business sector as the business-to-consumer. Research by Sirius in the UK in 2013 found that business consumers were typically 57 per cent of the way through their purchase process before they contacted suppliers. The same research found that 45 per cent of business consumers had already consulted the Internet before speaking to the potential supplier, 24 per cent had spoken to team members and colleagues about supplier options, 21 per cent had discussed options with a peer and 11 per cent had accessed online communities for reviews.

Take Time to Consider the Future

We hope this chapter has provoked some different thinking about customers' needs in the futue.

As a service leader it is important to take time to consider how things need to change to meet the future needs of the customer and also unmet and currently expressed needs. The challenge is to rise above the day to day and to look forward in an innovative way to prepare for the future. To start this process, ask yourself, your team, your peers, your boss, your customers:

- What future trends will impact us most in the next three to five years?

- What will customers particularly value about our service in the future?

- What aspects of the product/service/experience we offer need to be completely different?

- Where are the opportunities for future growth?

The future depends on what we do in the present.

Matama Gandhi

Chapter 8
Consistently Consistent

In this chapter we look at the need for a consistent focus on the customer and what it takes to ensure that customer-centricity is part of your own DNA and the culture of your organization.

This is the last chapter in the book and as in other chapters, we include tips, examples and checklists to help you assess yourself and your organization as well as consolidating key learning points and practical actions.

You May be Enthusiastic Now, but How do you Sustain a Customer Focus?

If you look at those companies who continually rank high in terms of customer experience, they have several characteristics in common: John Lewis department stores in the UK and companies like Nordstrom in the US are consistently reliable and in the service they deliver and customers can depend on them to consistently deliver a great service.

This does not happen by chance and it takes a lot of determined effort and focus. We often find that companies begin a journey to service excellence and then, after eighteen months to three years, the 'programme' dies and is replaced by another initiative. This is sometimes not helped by changes in leadership at the top of the organization or changes in strategic direction. Other times apathy sets in after an initial enthusiasm and customer centricity is not reinforced or given the importance that it once was as other priorities take shape.

DON'T REST ON YOUR LAURELS

We believe the most difficult part of customer leadership is consistently being consistent about the need for a great customer and employee experience, how you to continue to focus on this and the actions you take as a leader.

Best practice companies do not see customer experience as a one-off 'campaign' or 'initiative'. For them customer care is a way of life, it is part of the culture of the organization. These businesses continually measure and monitor customer satisfaction and benchmark themselves against the competition. They ensure that improvements are made in the levels of service that they give on an ongoing basis. After all, customer expectations are constantly increasing. What is best practice today will not be so in the future.

An example of on-going commitment is BMW in the UK. Their ambition is to be the number one car retailer of choice for both sales and service. It recognizes that it is on a journey that does not end and although it is making great progress in winning customer advocacy, each year it needs to do more. Their journey has included consistent setting standards for the customer journey in each retail outlet, a focus on leadership and behaviours, ongoing training, making improvements in the retail network to the way team members interact with customers and improving the processes that are used, developing a customer service recognition scheme for the retail network, creating a public online sales and service rating system for each retail outlet where customers award ratings and leave comments and feedback as well as changing the reward scheme for retailers to reflect customer feedback and taking part in National Customer Service week.

The challenge for leaders is to project out eighteen months to two years' time and consider and plan for what you and your team will be doing to ensure that the customer is still the number one priority. At an organizational level this may involve building in regular reviews of your team's performance in relation to customer advocacy and involving your teams in developing and reviewing service improvement plans based on what is important to customers. We've also discussed in the last chapter the importance of anticipating future customer needs.

It can involve placing customer advocacy on executive and senior leaders' meeting agendas as well as integrating customer feedback into every meeting you hold with your team.

It also involves integrating the customer-centric behaviours into all your people processes such as your vision and values, competency framework, recruitment and induction processes, objective setting and performance appraisal, talent management, development plans and reward and recognition schemes.

REPEAT YOUR MESSAGE

Remember that to change and reinforce a culture, you need to communicate again and again. Stay on message. Once is not enough. Show via your actions that how people treat the customer really matters.

Organizations such as the award-winning health care provider, the Mayo Clinic in the US, know that constant reinforcement is needed to ensure that everyone throughout the organization brings their vison to life. The organization's credo is '*The best interest of the patient is the only interest to be considered*'. This credo guides decisions everyday within the clinic. Care is focused around customer needs and there is strong and consistent evidence that patient's care is organized around their requirements. This means that doctor's schedules and hospital processes are focused on what is important to the patient rather than any other factors related to internal operations.

The clinic recognizes that every member of staff has an impact on the customer experience. It found from patient focus groups for example that their perception of the service they receive was as much impacted by their interaction with orderlies and cleaners as it was with clinical staff. All the leadership team, managers and staff undertake core customer training once a year where the expectations and experiences of patients are discussed. In addition each department creates service improvement plans, involving their customers in validating their actions. The feeling-of pride, accompanied with the alignment of employee attitudes, contribute to lower staff turnover: 4 per cent for nurses versus 20 per cent as an industry average.

Ten Top Tips for Sustaining a Customer Focus

1. Bring the voice of the customer in to the organization. Spend time with the customer and see the organization from the customer's perspective: by experiencing the service and ensuring the structure, systems and procedures make the organization easy to do business with. One international airline set up a special programme of visits where their senior executives accompanied their top customers on business trips using the airline. This was to allow senior managers to experience the service from the customer's perspective.

2. Co-create with customers. Nationwide Building Society uses customer panels to help develop every aspect of its products and

services. Companies from Pizza Hut to Lego are seeing the benefits of crowdsourcing and co-creating with customers. Consider how you can engage customers in improving your service – from including them on recruitment panels to having them judge recognition schemes to designing new service experiences.

3.   Encourage an external perspective and use it to embrace change: by benchmarking against best practice, attending customer service conferences and belong to a benchmarking forum. Award-winning Brazilian industrialist Ricardo Semler, President of Semco S/A consults with many major companies to compare effectiveness and believes that the main lesson businesses can learn is not to fear innovation but to lead change.

4.   Set high standards and be consistent about expecting these are met. Concierge company Ten Group operates on a global basis. Its customers expect an exceptional level of service and the CEO and the management team are uncompromising in terms of the standards they in turn expects of its team members. Deliver regular top-ups of training to help reinforce standards and to flex to customers' needs. Retailer the Arcadia Group ran a series of development sessions called 'A Sale is a Sale' to help all the employees in its head office and the retail network increase their awareness of the changing pattern of sales from bricks and mortar to online. The sessions generated thousands of ideas which were disseminated in to action plans about the role everyone across the business could play to better serve the customer.

5.   Recognize that employee engagement results in good external care, so spend time getting the people side of things right and spending time with your team. At Merrill Lynch Credit Corporation senior managers set the direction and tone for the company. They arrange quarterly meetings with all their employees (called partners) and support regular cross-functional training and continuous interaction with partners at all levels.

6.   Be visible and accessible. Spend time with teams; hold open forums; welcome feedback; work at the sharp end. Senior managers in organizations such as Marriott Hotels regularly spend time working in the hotels.

7.   Openly support customer care initiatives: by making time, money and resources available to them, attending events, leading improvement groups, making sure that customer care is on every management agenda. When one retail chain set out to improve its customer experience, senior managers took an active role in developing the programme and visiting stores to offer encouragement. The result was that employees knew that customer care was being taken seriously and that their contribution mattered. This led to a marked improvement in customer focus.

8.   Use social networks, both externally to gain insights into customer behaviour and internally to tap in to the growing use of collaboration and communication tools. Start a personal blog featuring your insights and interactions with customers.

9.   Measure and monitor levels of customer satisfaction, using feedback to take corrective action. Be accountable for this too. At the Chubb Group of insurance companies a variety of customer feedback programmes play a key role in balancing business success with a feeling of personal accomplishment.

10.   Recognize and reward excellent service. In the UK hi-fi retailer Richer Sounds has a customer experience competition each month and the winning three branches get to use a Bentley car for the month. They have seven holiday homes for people to use completely free of charge, irrespective of length of service or seniority. All senior managers are an integral part of this service reward process.

Do you Measure Up?

- Do customers lose out in the clutter of other priorities facing your senior managers? Test your senior management team (and yourself) to find out.

- Honestly rate customer contact against your other priorities: financial; shareholders; regulatory requirements; internal stakeholders. How would you rank these, in order?

- When did you last speak to a customer?

- Did you implement what you learned?

- How do you know what problems your people encounter when dealing with customers?

- When did you last update this knowledge?

- What is the gap between your organization's intended service strategy and how you really deal with the customer?

- Have you reviewed your organizational structure specifically for its customer orientation?

- Where do customer-facing employees sit in the hierarchy?

- What messages does your leadership style send to the customer and the rest of the organization?

- What feedback do you have to support this?

- How do you support and strengthen your staff's abilities to deal successfully with customers?

- Are your skills in giving and receiving feedback up to scratch?

- Do you use them regularly?

- Are you willing to tackle your colleagues about difficult issues which impede customer experience?

- Are the systems you operate likely to encourage customer satisfaction?

- Are reward and motivation systems linked up correctly with this aim?

Influencing Change in Your Organization

Become a change-maker for customers. In order to drive improvements in customer and employee engagement, take stock of your current organizational culture, what needs to be changed to work better for the customer and who you need to influence to ensure this is change.

Organizational culture is the personality of the organization, 'the way we do things around here'. Originally an anthropological term, culture refers to the underlying values, beliefs and codes of practice that make a business what it is. Management psychologist Schein describes culture as a phenomenon that surrounds us all. Culture according to Schein in his book *Organisational Culture and Leadership* is 'A pattern of shared basic assumptions that a group learns as it solves problems.'

It can be seen through:

1.   Behaviour: language, customs, traditions

2.   Groups norms: standards and values

3.   Espoused values: published, publicly announced values

4.   Formal philosophy: mission

5.   Rules of the game: rules to all in organizations

6.   Climate: climate of group in interaction

7.   Embedded skills

8.   Habits of thinking, acting, paradigms: shared knowledge for socialization

9.   Shared meanings of the group

10.   Metaphors or symbols.

Increasingly business leaders are recognizing that the concept of organizational culture is particularly important when it comes to changing the customer experience. If change is to be deep-seated and long-lasting within an organization, it needs to happen at a cultural level. The challenge for many organizations is how to change existing cultures because culture is rooted deep in the unconscious but represented in behaviour and practice.

The best way to begin a culture-change process is to better understand the culture in which you are currently operating. If you don't understand and manage culture, it will manage you. Be aware that there may be different types of culture operating within the same organization or part of an organization.

METHODS FOR ANALYSING ORGANIZATIONAL CULTURE

One way to understand culture is to use an analytical framework. Johnson and Scholes call their framework the Culture Web, a series of overlapping aspects of culture which make up the collective mind set. The Culture Web is best considered individually and then discussed with groups of managers. For example, look at your own organization in relation to the following:

- Symbols – logos, offices, cars

- Power – who has power

- Organizational structure – formal and informal structures

- Controls – what gets measured and rewarded

- Rituals – what are accepted procedures and rituals

- Stories – sometimes called 'war stories'.

There are a number of useful questionnaires which you can use to audit your company's culture. Completed by a cross-section of employees, they help to form a map of the context in which you are operating. In practice large and geographically spread businesses have many different types of cultures. Figure 8.1 is an example of a culture audit developed for an organization that wanted to assess its degree of customer orientation at the beginning of a culture change programme.

Circle the degree of your agreement in response to each statement.	Agree strongly 1	Agree 2	Disagree 3	Disagree Strongly 4
The most important aspect of our business is satisfying customers	1	2	3	4
Everybody has a customer - be it inside the organization or outside	1	2	3	4
We have 'heroes' who champion the customer	1	2	3	4
Our organization is not bureaucratic	1	2	3	4
Customers say we're special		2	3	4
The majority of people provide a high quality of service	1	2	3	4
Customer experience is a key corporate objective	1	2	3	4
You've got to talk the language of the customer to fit in round here	1	2	3	4
We recruit people whose attitude is orientated towards the customer	1	2	3	4
People work together as a team to serve the customer	1	2	3	4
Most of the stories which circulate seem to feature customers	1	2	3	4
Customer care is evident at Head Office as well as at the front-line	1	2	3	4
Our leaders demonstrate their enthusiasm for the customer	1	2	3	4
We are constantly finding new ways to satisfy our customers	1	2	3	4
We reward people for going out of their way for the customer	1	2	3	4
We encourage our customers to tell us if things are not right	1	2	3	4
We're always taking steps to implement new ideas to help the customer	1	2	3	4
Our systems and processes work smoothly	1	2	3	4
My manager sets a positive example in serving the customer	1	2	3	4
We talk about the customer in largely positive terms	1	2	3	4
I have been given training in knowledge, attitudes and skills which help us satisfy the customer	1	2	3	4
My personal objectives revolve around customer satisfaction	1	2	3	4
We have a clear understanding of the needs of our customers	1	2	3	4
Everyone is encouraged to ask for and act on feedback from	1	2	3	4

Figure 8.1   Customer Orientation Culture Audit

Now total your scores. Total: _____

The statements included in the questionnaire have been developed from research about what makes excellent customer-focused organizations. You can circulate the questionnaire to different parts of the organization and ask employees at all levels to complete it. The questionnaire can also act as a spring board for employee focus groups to share different perceptions of strengths and weaknesses in terms of service.

An alternative approach is to use a card-sort exercise. Descriptions are written on card to describe the way the organization works and what it values. The words on the card have negative as well as positive connotations, for example:

- Valuing diversity

- Working long hours

- Focusing on the customer

Groups of employees are invited to sort the cards to best describe what is important in the organization currently (i.e. what is the current culture). The resulting card sort creates a picture of the prevailing culture. The exercise can be repeated to focus on what employees would like the culture of the organization to be in the future. In this way a gap analysis can be undertaken between current and desired culture.

A further method is the use of rich pictures (so called because they provide rich metaphors about the organization). Here individuals are asked to depict the organization symbolically as if it was an image such as a body or a house or a mode of transport. Each person then describes why they have chosen to represent the organization in this way. The resulting discussions help tease out the way things are done in the organization.

Changing Culture

Most management gurus recognize that changing culture is a long-term project: it takes between three and five years. It is a process that can be undertaken bottom-up but ultimately very much depends on the leadership of the organization. When we say leaders we mean everyone throughout the organization who is in a position to lead others. As we have seen you, as part of this group, shape and reinforce the way that the organization functions.

It is generally accepted that to bring about culture change, all aspects of the organization need to change.

7 'S' FRAMEWORK

The 7 'S's diagnostic framework, developed by management consultants McKinsey, provides a useful perspective with which to assess the culture and effectiveness of an organization. The Seven 'S's are:

1. Structure

2. Strategy

3. Shared values

4. Style

5. Staff

6. Skills

7. Systems

1. Structure

There are many permutations of structure that an organization can adopt:

- Centralized

- Decentralized

- Hierarchical

- Flat

- Team-based

- Virtual

Each has its pros and cons. For example many layers of hierarchy can block a leader's access to customers and vice versa. Middle managers may 'filter' reality and present leaders with the picture of customer satisfaction which they wish them to see. The result of this is not only leaders who lack customer focus, but also employees who are fearful of 'stepping out of line' or taking responsibility for the customer.

2. Strategy

The strategy of an organization shapes its structure. Likewise the behaviours and values of an organization can promote or undermine its strategy.

3. Shared Values

If you discover the passion of the CEO, you will discover the organization's real priorities. Is there fundamental passion towards:

- making money?

- staff relationships?

- customer orientation?

These are important issues to get to the bottom of. What measures are used in reward systems? This often also shows the reality of what is important to the organization.

4. Style

How leaders behave influences the behaviours of their staff. We have talked about leadership style in earlier chapters and how the most effective leaders both support and challenge. They are sensitive to people's needs at the same time as inspiring the team to achieve the task. When senior managers' career paths have been via specialist or technical functions, for example, they may well fail to appreciate the need for a holistic approach to change. Typically where this style prevails, quantitative measures are set for operational delivery. Little attention is paid to the qualitative aspects of service, such as emotional intelligence, creating rapport and being empathetic to the customer.

Senior managers are often preoccupied with other influences such as competitors, shareholders, the City, government and regulatory bodies.

Customers compete against these other preoccupations for their share of airtime and often lose. Senior managers can all too easily become cocooned in a world far removed from the customer and the company people who work at the sharp end. One acid test of how removed your senior people may be from customers is: Who replies when a customer writes to the CEO?

This remoteness frequently leads managers to:

- Become hooked into the internal politics of the organization

- Shut off from honest feedback

- Rarely see the customer face-to-face.

This can all add up to management decisions which are far from customer-friendly, such as rules and regulations that work well for the organization but not the customer.

5. Staff

The need for engagement of employees as well as customers means that there is a trend to move front-line employees from a dependent, compliant and rule-bound group towards one where they freely take risks and confidently exercise discretion. As we have seen, people working for a taskmaster-style manager who is directive and autocratic develop into cynics – those who are reluctant or resistant to change, or spectators – who take a back seat when it comes to resolving a customer problem. This is because people often become resentful or discouraged to take initiative when they are constantly told what to do and when the only feedback they receive is negative.

New recruits soak up culture like sponges: they may have been recruited for their winning qualities, but they are influenced strongly by other's behaviours.

6. Skills

Customer-orientated organizations such as the department store Nordstrom in the US emphasize the attitude and interpersonal skills needed to interact effectively with customers. Role, skills and knowledge can be taught, whereas many of the less tangible, empathetic interpersonal skills involve being able to create vital rapport with customers. Nordstrom recruit only self-starters – a high commission system helps deselect others. Each of Nordstrom's 35,000 staff effectively runs their own business (within limited rules). Nordstrom's customer service is legendary, from its liberal return policy that allows customers to return items without a receipt to efforts by employees to make a connection with customers. Thank you cards, home deliveries, personal appointments and phone calls alerting customers of upcoming sales are all the norm at Nordstrom.

7. Systems

The systems which organizations use to interact with their customers need to be designed with the customer in mind. We talked earlier about the need to challenge processes and ways of working that take too much customer effort and the use of customer journey mapping techniques to help achieve this.

Customer Orientation Health Check

Changing organizational culture requires a long-term approach: it involves reassessing and making changes to all aspects of the organization. Use the following questions, based on the seven S framework, to assess the context in which you operate.

STRUCTURE

Have you reviewed your organizational structure specifically for its customer orientation?

Where do customer-facing employees sit in the hierarchy?

How internally customer-focused are your business support functions?

STRATEGY

Honestly rate the importance of customer-centricity against your other priorities: financial; shareholders; regulatory external; internal stakeholders. How would you rank these, in order?

1.

2.

3.

4.

5.

What is the gap between your organization's intended customer strategy and how you really deal with the customer?

SHARED VALUES

What is really important in your organization?

What should be important?

When did you last speak to a customer?

Did you implement what you learned?

STYLE

What messages does your leadership style send to the customer and the rest of the organization?

What feedback do you have to support this?

How do you support and strengthen your team's abilities to deal successfully with customers?

STAFF

How do you know what problems your people encounter when dealing with customers?

When did you last update this knowledge?

SKILLS

What skills development have you had in the past 12 months to better serve the customer?

Are your skills in giving and receiving feedback up to scratch?

Do you use them regularly?

Are you willing to tackle your colleagues about difficult issues which impede great customer service?

SYSTEMS

Are the systems you operate likely to encourage customer satisfaction?

Are reward and motivation systems linked up correctly with this aim?

We hope that the answers to these questions will help you gauge where your organization needs to change and that you can engage your team, peers and line managers in creating a plan of action for how to do this.

Summary

Our wish is that by reading this book you have the appetite and the energy to drive improvement in employee and customer engagement in your organization. We would like to close this book with the offer of contacting us for follow-up advice if you need it and by giving you two quotes to consider going forward:

> *Service is not what you do, but who you are. It is a way of living that you need to bring to everything you do. Betsy Sanders*

> *The longer you wait, the harder it is to produce outstanding customer service. William H. Davidow*

Bibliography

A National Customer Satisfaction Barometer: The Swedish Experience, *Journal of Marketing*, 56 (1), Fornell C., 1992.

Aon Hewitt European Manager Survey, 2011, Aon Hewitt,London.

Average to A+: Realising Strengths in Yourself and Others (Strengthening the World Series), Linley A., 2008, CAPP Press, London.

Buyer Intention to Use Internet-enabled Reverse Auctions: The Role of Asset Specificity, Product Specialization, and Non-contractibility, *MIS Quarterly*, 32 (4), Mithas S., Jones J.L. and Mitchell W., 2008.

Character Strengths and Virtues: A Handbook and Classification, Peterson C., 2004, Oxford University Press, Oxford.

Change Management Excellence, Cook S., Macaulay S. and Coldicott H., 2004, Kogan Page, London.

Complaint Management Excellence, Cook S., 2012, Kogan Page, London.

Contagious Customer Care, Frisby N., 2001, Go MAD Books, London.

Customer Care Excellence, Cook S., 2010, Kogan Page, London.

Customer Centered Six Sigma: Linking Customers, Process Improvement, And Financial Results, Naumann E. and Hoisington S., 2001, ASQ Quality Press, Milwaukee, Wisconsin.

Customer Satisfaction and Shareholder Value, *Journal of Marketing*, 68 (4), Anderson E.W., Fornell C. and Mazvancheryl S.K., 2004.

Customer Satisfaction, Market Share, and Profitability: Findings from Sweden, *Journal of Marketing*, 58 (3), Anderson E.W., Fornell C. and Lehmann D.R., 1994.

Driving Performance and Retention Through Employee Engagement: A Quantitative Analysis of Effective Engagement Strategies, 2004, Corporate Leadership Council, London.

Employee Empowerment: The Rhetoric and the Reality, Huq R., 2010, Triarchy Press, Axminster.

Employee Engagement (HR Fundamentals), Bridger E., 2014, Kogan Page, London.

Employee Engagement in Theory and Practice, Truss C. and Alfes K., 2013, Routledge, Abingdon.

Employee Engagement: Tools for Analysis, Practice, and Competitive Advantage, Macey W.H., Schneider B., Barbera K.M. and Young S.A., 2009, Wiley-Blackwell, Oxford.

Engaged: Unleashing Your Organization's Potential Through Employee Engagement, Holbeche L. and Matthews G., 2012, Jossey-Bass, San Francisco.

European Talent Survey: Reconnecting with Employees: Attracting, Retaining, and Engaging, Towers Perrin, 2004, Towers Perrin, London.

Five Star Service: How to Deliver Exceptional Customer Service (Prentice Hall Business), Heppell M., 2010, Pearson Business, London.

Friends, Following and Feedback How We're Using Social Media, Online September, 2011, Nielsen.

Global advertising: Consumers Trust Real Friends and Virtual Strangers most, 2009, Nielsen Wire, New York.

Hiring for Attitude: A Revolutionary Approach to Recruiting and Selecting People with Both Tremendous Skills and Superb Attitude, Murphy M., 2011, McGraw-Hill Professional Publishing, New York The book was published in 2011 (2012 in ch 5 at the moment). There was a white paper published in 2012.

Hiring for Attitude: Research and Tools to Skyrocket your Success Rate, Murphy M., 2012, Leadership IQ Whitepaper, Washington DC.

How. Full is your Bucket? Rath T. and Clifton D., 2004, Gallup Press, New York.

How will Demographic Trends Affect the Retail Sector, KPMG/Ipsos Retail Think Tank, 2014, London.

Investors Take Note:Engagement Boosts Earnings, Ott B. 14 June 2007, Business Journal.

Innovation Management: Strategy and Implementation using the Pentathlon Framework, Goffin K., 2005, Palgrave Macmillan, Basingtoke.

Leadership & Organizational Climate, Stringer A., 2002, Prentice Hall, London.

Linking People Measures to Strategy, Gates S., 2003, Conference Board, New York.

Managing Innovation: Integrating Technological, Market and Organizational Change, Tidd J., 2013 JohnWiley & Sons, Chichester.

Managing Quality: The Strategic and Competitive Edge, Garvin, D.A., 1988, Free Press, New York.

Marketing Assets and the Value of Customer Assets. A Framework for Customer Asset Management, *Journal of Service Research*, 5 (1), Berger P.D., Bolton R.N., Bowman D., Briggs E., Kumar V., Parasuraman A. and Creed T., 2002.

Organisational Culture and Leadership, 3rd edition, Schein, E, 2006, Jossey Bass, San Franscisco.

Psychology of Customer Care: A Revolutionary Approach, Lynch H.E., 1992, Palgrave Macmillan , Basingstoke.

Relating Brand and Customer Perspectives on Marketing Management, *Journal of Service Research*, 5 (1), Ambler T., Bhattacharya C.B., Edell J., Keller K.L., Lemon K.N. and Mittalv V., 2002.

Reward Management: Employee Performance, Motivation and Pay, Hume D., 1995, Blackwell Business, Oxford.

Strategic Management ,Vordbera H., 2011, Cengage Learning, EMEA, Andover.

SuperMotivation: A Blueprint for Energizing Your Organization from Top to Bottom, Spitzer, D, 1995, AMACOM, New York *Technical Paper, Q12® Meta-Analysis,*

Harter, J.K., Schmidt, F.L., Killham, E.A. and Asplund, J. W, 2006, Gallup Organization, Omaha Nebraska.

The Art of Empowerment: The Profit and Pain of Employee Involvement, Johnson R. and Redmond D., 1998, Financial Times Pitman, London.

The Art of Possibility: Transforming Professional and Personal Life, Zander R.S. and Zander B., 2002, Penguin Books, London.

The Culture Engine: A Framework for Driving Results, Inspiring Your Employees, and Transforming Your Workplace, Edmonds S.C., 2014, John Wiley & Sons, Oxford.

The Employee-organization Relationship, Organizational Citizenship Behaviours, and Superior Service Quality, *Journal of Retailing*, 78 (2), Bell S.J. and Menguc B., 2002.

The Essential Guide to Employee Engagement: Better Business Performance through Staff Satisfaction, Cook S., 2008, Kogan Page, London.

The Loyalty Elephant, Customer Satisfaction, Quality Progress, 2003, Hoisington S. and Naumann E. February Vol. 2.

The Relationship Between Engagement at Work and Organizational Outcomes, Q12® Meta-Analysis, 2012, Harter J.K., Schmidt F.L., Agrawal S. and Plowman S.K., 2013, Gallup Organization, Omaha Nebraska.

The Service Profit Chain: How Leading Companies Link Profit and Growth to Loyalty, Satisfaction, and Value, Heskett J., Sasser W.E. and Schlesinger L.A., 1997, The Free Press, New York.

The Ten Principles Behind Great Customer Experiences (Financial Times Series), Watkinson M., 2012, FT Publishing International, London.

Understanding the Challenges of Dealing with Informed, Demanding and Networked Customers, The Autonomous Customer, 2011, Avaya and BT, BT Global Services, London.

US Technical Assistance Research Program Studies, 2006, Executive Blueprints Inc, New York.

Working with Emotional Intelligence, D. Goleman, 1999, Bloomsbury, London.

Index

If you have found this book useful you may be interested in other titles from Gower

The Culture Builders
Leadership Strategies for Employee Performance
Jane Sparrow
9781409437246 (paperback)
9781409437253 (e-book – PDF)
9781409483922 (e-book – ePUB)

Effective Client Management in Professional Services
How to Build Successful Client Relationships
Jack Berkovi
9781409437895 (hardback)
9781409437901 (e-book – PDF)
9781472407986 (e-book – ePUB)

What the New Breed of CMOs Know That You Don't
MaryLee Sachs
9781409455721 (hardback)
9781409455738 (e-book – PDF)
9781472404046 (e-book – ePUB)

The Irrational Consumer
Applying Behavioural Economics to Your Business Strategy
Enrico Trevisan
9781472413444 (hardback)
9781472413451 (e-book – PDF)
9781472413765 (e-book – ePUB)

Visit **www.gowerpublishing.com** and

- search the entire catalogue of Gower books in print
- order titles online at 10% discount
- take advantage of special offers
- sign up for our monthly e-mail update service
- download free sample chapters from all recent titles
- download or order our catalogue